REALIZING GOD'S VISION
OF FUTURE SOCIETY

Faithful
to the
Truth

HS PRESS

REALIZING GOD'S VISION
OF FUTURE SOCIETY

Faithful
to the
Truth

EL CANTARE

Ryuho Okawa

HS PRESS

Contents

CHAPTER ONE

Faithful to the Truth

CHAPTER TWO

Making the Way to
True Salvation

CHAPTER THREE

Overcoming the Crisis of Earth
—A Lecture on *The Laws of Hell*

CHAPTER ONE

Faithful to the Truth

Originally recorded in Japanese on November 20, 2022
at Special Head Temple Holy Land El Cantare Seitankan
in Tokushima, Japan
and later translated into English.

1

What I Believe to Be the Truth
at This Moment

The Laws of Hell that teaches how to deal with hell is a must-read

This lecture marks the 36th anniversary of the First Turning of the Wheel of Truth. Time flew by so fast. Recently, I watched some of the lectures I gave about 30 years ago because they are currently made available for our members to watch at our local temples. The energy and spirit I had back then reminded me of how good it is to be in the 30s. But at the same time, I feel that it is also good to be a little aged and ripe.

I have heard that the average age of my audience today at this main venue (Special Head Temple Holy Land El Cantare Seitankan) is 59.3 years old, so you probably expect me to give a talk on a much deeper topic than a young person's love story. (Editor's Note: Before the lecture, a song titled, "Love After Ten Years" was sung.) The majority of you have probably lived through most of life's events, so even if I talk about how to live through life, perhaps it might be too late for you to learn about it now [*audience laughs*]. "A little too late" might be more appropriate, so you may have to carry over your problems to the next life.

Next year (2023), we will publish a book called *The Laws of Hell* (New York: IRH Press, 2023). This is an extremely important book. I recommend that you place a copy of it in your coffin when you go. I hope you will read it while you are still alive, but if you are not able to read it thoroughly enough, please take it with you in your coffin. This book is a must-read because it teaches how to deal with hell. It is priceless and very important. Perhaps I should be happy that I have reached an age where I can say such things.

What I think of the current situation surrounding religion

Since the summer of this year (2022), the situation surrounding religion in Japan has not been very good. The relationship between religion, politics, and mass media has been quite bad. Issues concerning them usually emerge all of a sudden, so I have been having bad feelings all along. When there are over 180,000 religious groups in Japan, it is normal to find strange ones among them, so I want to believe that people are not as foolish to think that religions are all the same. That is why Happy Science activities have been so reserved.

Most people are vaguely aware of the differences between religions, but unfortunately, there are currently no religious scholars or politicians who can point this out; neither can journalists clearly state their differences. That is why, when a certain religious group causes problems, either all religions are praised or all religions are criticized as a whole. We are quite troubled by this tendency.

Thirty years ago, we experienced something of the sort. When Happy Science became quickly well-known, other religious groups tried to jump on the bandwagon and started publicizing themselves as well. But as soon as one religious group got criticized, all other groups, including Happy Science, were put in the same boat and dragged down altogether. I remember we had a hard time.

I always believe I must say what needs to be said, but I have to be careful not to overdo it because the "bullets" might come back at us. This wisdom comes with age, and this is something young people do not have. What I now do is use various ways to express what I need to say, such as saying it in a roundabout way or writing it in my novels[1]. I try not to be as straightforward as I was 30 years ago.

Today's lecture is, "Faithful to the Truth." I chose this title for the following reasons. Japanese people, in general, tend to change their opinions altogether when an incident happens. In a given situation, they drastically change or flip their opinions from one side to the other or from good to bad. The same is true with the United States. The direction of the country changes depending on whether the Republicans or Democrats win the election. Under such fluid circumstances, it is quite hard to teach the eternal Laws or the unchanging Truth. I do feel that I should adapt more to the trends of society to a certain extent. But even so, I believe there are some basics that must never be changed.

In Japan, how religion is treated changes from very well to very poor, and this makes things difficult for us. Politics may have power in a practical sense, but for religion, its fundamental role is authority. So, religion must speak out from the position of authority, and by doing so, influence people of various leadership positions in society. I believe this is the basic standpoint that Happy Science should take for the time being. For this reason, it is important for me to speak about what I believe is the truth at this moment and tell people how they should think from now on.

I have two more lectures in mind; one that will be given at the El Cantare Celebration in Saitama Super Arena on December 6 (compiled as Chapter Two) and another at the beginning of next year, "*The Laws of Hell Seminar*" (compiled as Chapter Three). Much like the State of the Union Address, the three lectures, including today's one, will provide you with Happy Science's basic ideas and activity policies for next year (2023). So today's lecture will play an important part. This venue is rather packed, so I will speak calmly today so as not to blow you out of the hall [*audience laughs*]. I will give my full-blown lecture at Saitama Super Arena instead.

Today's lecture is my 3,480th one. We recorded a brief "UFO reading" last night ("UFO Reading No. 71: Metatron"), so if we count that in, this lecture will be the 3,480th one. With only 20 more, the number will reach 3,500. Even after all these lectures, because the topics are so vast, my basic messages have not reached the whole world yet. But I am the only one who can preach about what I talk about, so I feel I have to say what must be said.

EDITOR'S NOTE

1 Novels include *Shousetsu Naimen e no Michi* (lit. "Novel: The Path to the Inner World"), *Shousetsu Harukanaru Ihoujin* (lit. "Novel: A Stranger from Afar"), *Shousetsu Yuragi* (lit. "Novel: Fluctuation") and *Shousetsu Tottchimete Yaranakucha* (lit. "Novel: I Have to Give Her a Scolding") (all Tokyo: Happy Science, 2022). Available only in Japanese.

2

The Problems of Today's Society

The importance of teaching the "enlightenment of the whole"

Let me first tell you my main message today. In the First Turning of the Wheel of Truth Session (November 23, 1986), I said that I would be talking about the teachings to attain the "enlightenment of the individual" and the "enlightenment of the whole." The enlightenment of the individual means the wisdom to change yourself by learning and understanding how you should live as a human being. A considerable amount of my teachings are of this wisdom. Especially, while our organization was still small, this wisdom was our main focus.

However, now that our organization has grown to a certain size, we have to put more emphasis on talking about the enlightenment of the whole, that is to say, the topics that would impact the entire world, such as the ideal state of a nation, the structure of the universe, and the relationship between this world and the Spirit World.

I have the duty to teach those things also. Even though there are other major world religions, their teachings are old and they do not cover everything. They do not teach about the right way to view the world, and in many cases, the old teachings do not allow people to judge whether the events happening now are right or wrong. I believe it is very important that religions can provide answers to every problem in real time.

The Japanese Constitution guarantees many kinds of freedom, including freedom of speech, freedom of thought or belief, freedom of religion, and freedom of the press. They are all certainly important. We, too, have benefited from them and are able to publish many books thanks to them, so these kinds of freedom are good. However, if wrong opinions spread too widely because of these freedoms, that is a problem. For the right to persuade the wrong, those in the right will need stronger words and stronger power.

I do not mean to assert self-righteous opinions. For example, here in Shikoku, esoteric Shingon Buddhism taught by Kobo-Daishi Kukai is a major religion and it has many temples, but I am not stating my opinion with the intention of putting their temples out of business.

If we trace back the origin of Kukai's faith, we can find Mahavairocana Buddha at the source of Shingon Buddhism or esoteric Buddhism. Mahavairocana Buddha can be regarded as the being who first taught the teachings that became the basis of esoteric Buddhism. Mahavairocana Buddha is the part of Buddha's soul that preaches the Truth. The source of Kukai's teachings, the Truth, flows directly from Mahavairocana Buddha, so his teachings are genuine and are neither wrong nor different.

Moreover, when the focus is placed on salvation, the power of Amitabha Buddha is mainly at work. Many Buddhist schools that practice chanting are under this power; they focus on saving people. When I give my teachings, I use these two aspects of Buddha accordingly. Sometimes, I focus on the Amitabha Buddha aspect and teach salvation, and sometimes I focus on the Mahavairocana Buddha aspect and teach the Truth.

Today, I believe I must focus more on the teachings that relate more to Mahavairocana Buddha, but I do not intend for Shingon temples to go bankrupt at all. Rather, I hope they will adopt the teachings of Happy Science and have stronger conviction in the Truth.

There are also many Shinto shrines, but I have no intention of destroying them, either. Japanese Shinto only has a torii gate and not many teachings, so I would be grateful if they would supplement it with our teachings.

Make constant efforts to discover and remove your false self

People have different needs, so first, I would like to talk a little about what I have been concerned about recently regarding an individual's way of living.

One is about a conceited mind. I raised this issue in our recent movie, *The Divine Protector—Master Salt Begins* (Executive Producer Ryuho Okawa, 2022). For its final climax, I chose to tell people about the importance of removing a tengu-type, conceited mindset, which is quite difficult to do. The desire for fame, arrogance, and boastfulness are the toughest to remove even for religious practitioners. When people believe that they are doing the right thing or studying the Truth, these thoughts can often make them look arrogant, conceited, or haughty in the eyes of others. You may appear as though you are saying, "I am the awakened one" or "All of you unawakened ones, listen carefully to what I say," so this is one thing people need to be very careful of.

Happy Science Group has a political party, and our staff working there must also be careful on this point. If they confuse politics for religion and make a self-assertive speech from a podium as if to say, "I'm an awakened one, so all of you listen carefully to what I have to say," then they will start to lose their audience. In this sense, how politics and religion should approach their audience is slightly different, so our political staff must know the difference and use them appropriately. As a political approach, they would need to make a speech in a way that gains the understanding and support of the listeners.

What I particularly want to emphasize today in relation to conceit is, as I have already taught you long ago, how to grasp your true self. In other words, I do not want you to stop making efforts to discover the false self that lies inside of you. Especially, when you grow older, your false self hardens considerably and becomes very tough to remove. It is as if the mask you are wearing hardens on your face and gets stuck that you cannot pull it off. Many factors contribute to developing a false self such as the fact that your name is well-known, you have a high social status, you work for a famous company, or you have a high educational background. Although it is natural for people to develop such false selves as they grow older, if their "masks" become stuck to their faces and cannot be removed, they will not be able to see things for how they are. In this way, as people grow older, they tend to have an inflexible mindset and find it hard to understand the ideas of young people or those of a different gender. So, even as you grow older, I want you to continuously make efforts to discover your false self. It is very important, even for people who are past their middle age, to constantly make efforts to find and remove their false selves.

Let me tell you why. There would not be so much of a problem if your false self is much like the makeup women wear, but if it becomes so solid to the point that it becomes part of your face, like a mask that you cannot take off, then evil spirits or malicious spirits will hook on this part to come and possess you. If you are in a position of power, devils are what will approach and possess you. So you need to be careful about this point.

The dangers of the idea that
"science is cutting-edge and almighty"

Recently, I have been studying Korean TV dramas because they are quite well-made. In South Korea, dramas about how to deal with people who have lost their minds due to spiritual possession are quite popular. At least, in terms of this spiritual aspect, you may feel that Korean TV dramas are a little more advanced than Japanese ones because spiritual matters seem to be more publicly available in South Korea. The TV programs in Japan do not go this deep, so in terms of faith, South Korean people may be more sincere, or perhaps more developed than Japanese people. Generally, everything in Japan has become a little more materialistic.

There is one thing we need to be especially careful of when society is in this kind of trend. Science developed significantly in the last 200 years, but religion has a much longer history than that. Even so, science is treated as if it is more cutting-edge and almighty compared to religion. President Biden also says this, but science is considered to be at the forefront. Those who deny scientific ideas are often labeled as unscientific or anti-science, and treated as superstitious or outdated people. I see some danger in this tendency.

Science came to the world after religion and is gradually spreading, permeating deeply into school education as well. So, people have started to strongly believe that anything that goes against science is neither the truth nor academic. Although there is some truth in this idea, Japan still has not managed to send an artificial satellite to the Moon. So really, it should not be so arrogant with such a level of science. They have not even managed to send a rocket to the Moon to explore it or have someone walk on its surface.

I, on the other hand, have already observed the other side of the Moon without physically moving [*audience laughs*], so I do feel that I am on a whole different level (refer to *Dark Side Moon no Enkaku Toushi* [lit. "Remote-Viewing of the Dark Side of the Moon," Tokyo: IRH Press, 2014], available only in Japanese). I am showing the truth from not a scientific but from a religious approach.

It is wrong to assume that a single academic field alone has the answers to everything and it is also wrong to lay the foundation of education on such an assumption. Especially after Japan's Ministry of Education took in the Science and Technology Agency and became the Ministry of Education, Culture, Sports, Science and Technology, people's understanding of religion has dropped significantly. This is not a good trend.

It is a preconception to think, "What is not scientific is not the truth." This is another form of brainwashing and a blind assumption. Science was originally all about finding the truth through the act of questioning various things and narrowing down the answers. But the problem now is that anything that is labeled "science" is in the right.

Take, for example, global warming. This phenomenon could be true, but it could also be false. What I mean by this is that the Earth used to be much warmer in the distant past. When dinosaurs existed, plants flourished to the level that there was enough food for such gigantic creatures to eat. Put simply, when the Earth was warmer, food, such as plants and animals, grew much bigger and this phenomenon enabled large creatures to survive. Therefore, this is not the first time Earth has been warm, so the natural disasters that have been occurring recently may not necessarily be caused by global warming only. Somewhere in our minds, we must be open to thinking that while global warming could be the cause, this possibility could also be wrong. It is a problem to assume that what one person says is all and everything.

What is considered "science" is not always right

Thinking back to the coronavirus pandemic, the first year was terrible. For example, it was hard to come into Tokushima Prefecture. Cars with license plates from other prefectures were banned from the streets of Tokushima, and if anyone was spotted, they were secretly reported to the police. It was unbelievable. It felt like we were back in the Edo period (1600s — 1800s). People of Tokushima were afraid just to see cars from other prefectures.

In the first year of the pandemic, we called a hotel in Tokushima from Tokyo to book rooms because I wanted to visit Iya Valley which I had not been to in a long time. But we were told, "We don't accept visitors from Tokyo." That was when I realized that they think we are germs. We told the hotel that we were originally from Tokushima, but they still declined us saying, "It doesn't matter. We don't accept visitors from Tokyo, since there are a lot of viruses there." Looking back now, the number of infected cases in Tokushima was very small. Only a handful were infected and there were "nil" infected cases in many prefectures in the Tohoku area (northeast Japan). But even so, they refused us. This left me with a "deep scar" [*audience laughs*].

But now, no one seems to care even when the virus is still going around and tens of thousands of people are still being infected daily. I saw on TV that foreign tourists from France were visiting Mima City in Tokushima, so the situation has changed drastically. I guess it really depends on how people think and feel. Tens of thousands of people are still being infected every year, every month, and every day, but now, three years after the outbreak (at the time of the lecture), people understand that the coronavirus is not so much different from the common cold or the flu.

In this sense, I kind of understand how former President Trump did not wear a mask and commented that the coronavirus was the same as the flu. He was criticized for saying things like, "Churches should stay open, especially in times like this," "We need people who pray to God," or "Don't close the churches saying that people would be infected if they go there." He was criticized and told he was unscientific or anti-science. In hindsight, however, he did not say anything that he should be condemned for.

In the initial stages of the pandemic in Japan, the governor of Tokyo was working so hard to impose many restrictions in an effort to prevent the spread of the coronavirus, but she now keeps her silence. She actually spent ¥1 trillion (about US$7 billion) in a year for the countermeasures against coronavirus. In just a year, she spent ¥1 trillion, which the former Governor Shintaro Ishihara worked hard to save, and now Tokyo is penniless. So, she is now keeping silent and working quietly to stay under the radar and avoid being held accountable for what she has done. She made too much of a fuss early on that now when the number of infected cases is much greater, she is out of things to say.

Things like this can happen. So, what I want to say is, science is technically made up of the opinions and theories of all kinds of people. Therefore, we never know whether the leader at a given point in time is saying the right thing or not. Rather than relying on the leader at the time, each person should return to the basics and make their own efforts. They should, once again, study and relearn various matters properly. I am not teaching you to be unscientific or anti-science. We are "Happy Science," so we absolutely have no intention of denying science. Even so, I will express my opinions clearly if I find something to be wrong. This includes topics that are considered scientific by the public.

3

The Righteousness as a Country

Happy Science has been raising warnings about the nuclear threat of North Korea from 30 years ago

After reading *The Laws of Hell*, all of you will probably think about what you can do to avoid falling to hell, or at least think of ways of falling only to the shallower part of hell so that you can return to heaven as quickly as possible. But at the same time, not everything is under our control. Sometimes the national or global economy or the negative impact brought by the economy, politics, or military affairs can affect where you will go after death. So, you need to study both perspectives. You must also be wary of ideas or policies that are likely to gain support from many people because they often stand against the Truth. In many cases, it takes some time for the public to have the same opinion as mine. It takes up to 10 to 30 years or sometimes even 50 years, so please be aware of this.

There is another thing I would like to mention today. After World War II, there were some minor wars, but relatively speaking, we have had a peaceful 80 years. Japanese people are fortunate that Japan did not wage war during this period. Also, those who were born and died during this period did not have to witness war, so they, indeed, lived through peaceful times. However, those of us who have several decades left to live will experience tough times from now on. I am sure you can get a sense of what I mean by this when you watch the news.

At the same time, there may be news that you will misunderstand or misinterpret. For example, although North Korea fires missiles and ballistic missiles so frequently, Japan does nothing and only says, "We protest it." To be honest, I want to tell the Japanese government that they must take action instead of simply "protesting." For 30 years, or since the 1990s, I have been giving warnings against North Korea's missiles, but only now have people started making a fuss about them. It makes me wonder whether the Japanese are truly civilized people. They are way behind the times.

We had already depicted the nuclear missile crisis by North Korea in our first movie, *The Terrifying Revelations of Nostradamus* (Executive Producer Ryuho Okawa, released in 1994). It was a hit, and the movie won some awards at the time, even from the *Asahi Shimbun Newspaper* for some reason. Usually, Asahi Shimbun's opinions are opposite of ours, but they gave us an award. Perhaps they thought the movie was mere entertainment or fantasy.

In the movie, there was a scene where a large demon-like creature appeared to symbolize the major threat of nuclear missiles from North Korea. We put this movie out in 1994. We began making it in 1991, so it's already been more than 30 years ago, but what has Japan been doing all these years? Nothing. People in Japan are really behind the times and are taking peace for granted.

Japanese people believe that "No more Hiroshima" is the common view in the world

There is another thing I want to tell you. Japanese people, including everyone here, people of the mass media, and also politicians, have a wrong preconception. Here is what I mean.

Nearly 80 years ago, the atomic bombs were dropped on Hiroshima and Nagasaki. So, Japanese people often claim, "We suffered such a tragedy," "No more atomic bombs. No more wars. No more Hiroshima," and they undoubtedly believe that the world also believes this as a common understanding. But this is not true.

The United States, which dropped the two atomic bombs, has never apologized or expressed remorse for what it did. This shows that their stance is still the same: they dropped the atomic bombs for the sake of justice and killed Japanese people, who they believed were more evil than the Native Americans. So, they still think that their atomic bombs can be used to realize justice.

What this entails is this. There are several countries in the world that have atomic and hydrogen bombs, including those that are not permanent members of the United Nations Security Council. If the first country that dropped atomic bombs admits that it was an inhumane act and all its citizens spend days in repentance with their heads shaved, then it will be unlikely for nuclear bombs to be used again. But in reality, the country has never repented for what it did. This means that other countries can claim their own justice as well.

Nevertheless, Japanese people blindly and optimistically believe that atomic bombs and hydrogen bombs will not be used. This is the majority of Japanese people. They think that these bombs should and would never be used again whatsoever. That is why, no matter how many times they hear about nuclear missiles on the news, it goes in one ear and out the other. They just think, "There's no way that atomic bombs will be dropped again" or "Reasonably speaking, there's no way it will happen again."

However, what they must know is that people of other countries do not share the same pain as Japan because they have never suffered from the dropping of atomic bombs. The people of other countries just assume, "Japan must have been an evil country. That's why the atomic bombs were dropped on them. Good for them." So, countries such as the U.S., Russia, North Korea, Pakistan, India, China, Israel, and perhaps Iran, too, in the near future, could use nuclear bombs for the sake of their own justice. Japanese people should know this. This is definitely not a biased opinion. While it is fine for Japanese people to keep chanting "No more Hiroshima" like a mantra, they must know that the world thinks differently. The people writing newspaper articles or reporting the news on TV in Japan may be giving the facts, but their interpretation and understanding could be wrong.

Nuclear war is an impending crisis

Objectively speaking, now, the world is under an impending crisis of a nuclear war. It has been quite a while since we last experienced it. You never know when North Korea may start a war. The latest ballistic missile from North Korea landed near an island in Hokkaido, so they are now shooting it within Japan's exclusive economic zone (EEZ). Their missiles used to land outside of it but now, they land within. Even then, Japan's response remains the same. So, North Korea might now be thinking, "Maybe we could shoot a missile on an uninhabited island or a sparsely inhabited area of Hokkaido." They may even be thinking, "We could shoot it into Tokyo Bay. It won't be a problem as long as it doesn't hit a vessel." In this way, their attacks could escalate, little by little, and at some point, Japan's patience will run out, although I am not sure how Japan will react at that time.

Currently, Taiwan and Japan are facing a similar crisis, and so is South Korea. The fact that even the members of the South Korean popular boy band BTS were finally drafted for mandatory military service means they must serve as role models for its citizens and they need to do more than just sing songs.

Also, the Russo-Ukrainian War continues to go on. Even so, Japanese people assume there is no way that nuclear weapons will ever be used. Other countries probably think so, too. They basically assume that Russia will continue to fight the war with "their hands tied," or in other words, without using nuclear weapons. In the meantime, countries are sending more and more supplies into Ukraine by saying that Russia is already running out of missiles, bombs, tanks, and aircraft. You can indeed support Ukraine, but sending more supplies means that the war will drag on and more people will die. Russia says that they will use nuclear weapons should they run out of conventional weapons—they are not bluffing, they really mean it. Since atomic bombs were allowed to be dropped on Japan, if worse comes to worst, Russia could also use them, just as they say they will. If the war reaches a point where Russia could truly perish or lose, Russia may use nuclear weapons.

Also, it recently became very clear to me that Mr. Zelensky of Ukraine is a liar. When a missile landed in Poland and killed two people, he said it was Russia who fired it. But the U.S. pointed out that, considering the direction in which the missile came from, it was obviously an interceptor missile fired from Ukraine. Even so, he insisted, "We can't confirm that. Russia is the only one who could've fired it." Russia may have been the indirect cause, but before Mr. Zelensky makes such accusations, he must understand that Ukraine has already sunk a Russian warship and destroyed Russian bridges, which could inevitably invite a full-scale attack by Russia. The fact that he does not understand this is an issue.

I am not sure whether Mr. Zelensky is at all a good person or not. He used to be a comedian, so he is good at manipulating how he is perceived by the public through TV. Russia is now gradually changing its attitude because its people are leaving the country. But Ukraine, on the other hand, does not allow adolescent males to leave the country. Since they are potential military personnel, they are all expected to die in battles. I wonder how far Mr. Zelensky wants to take this. If the leader of a nation does not know when to stop a war or when to concede or compromise, the damage will just get worse. He must consider when to put an end to this war.

Local regions must also function to maintain the country's ability to develop

In China, Mr. Xi Jinping is in his third term. If he fails to take over Taiwan during his third term, he probably will not be able to serve his fourth term. I think that is why China is forming closer ties with North Korea. In our spiritual messages, the guardian spirit of Mr. Xi Jinping said that when he takes over Taiwan, he will also take Japan. That is why the tension is building up around Ishigaki Island in Okinawa. But China's target may not necessarily be the island and they may attack somewhere else instead.

I am not a warmonger, of course, and I am not suggesting we should go to war. What I want to say is, "I've been giving warnings from 30 years ago, so the Japanese government should have taken me more seriously. If they had made preparations for it all these years, things could have been a bit better." Japan should be and is allowed to defend itself. So the Japanese government must act and protect the territory of the Japanese people, their airspace, human rights, and property.

While it is fine to raise the names of the politicians who negotiated with North Korea over the return of the Japanese abductees by North Korea, this is quite shameful for a sovereign nation. Japanese citizens were abducted from the seashores of Japan, but all that the Japanese government does is *ask* North Korea to return them. They even rely on the U.S. to negotiate with North Korea on their behalf. This is shameful. Japan should act properly and resolutely and do what it must do as a nation.

Nuclear missiles will most probably not be dropped on Tokushima (where this lecture was given). The population is so low here, so it would be a waste to target a place like this. One missile costs about a billion yen, so it is unlikely for such a scarcely populated area to be targeted. Places that have a population of a million people would usually be the main target, so the area around Tokushima will be safe.

My family lives in Minato Ward in Tokyo, which is close to an area where the Prime Minister's Office is located. Areas like Minato Ward and Chiyoda Ward will most likely be targeted. If these areas were to be destroyed, much of Japan's "brain" would be lost. Should these areas be bombarded intensively, Japan would stop functioning for a while. That is why I built the Special Head Temple in Tokushima. I want you all to survive in the case of an emergency. From now on, it may be more advantageous to live in rural areas.

The population of Tokushima has now decreased by 100,000 people compared to the time I used to live here, so I am a little sad. My alma mater, Jonan High School, used to be a high-level school, but no one knows about it now. It is sad. Although it used to be a prestigious school, nowadays, the only famous person other than me who is a graduate of the school is an occult researcher who is about 10 years younger than me. Apparently, he is aware that I graduated from the same school as him and considers me his senior. After me, my alma mater did not produce any successful person for a while, and 10 years later, the one who came was an occultist. An occultist after a religious leader; that's all there was. There are only a few graduates from my alma mater who are successful in the field of work that is considered conventional in society. This is a pity.

What I want to say is that we need to strongly promote the decentralization of power in the truest sense, so that local regions can also function to maintain Japan's vitality and ability to develop. There is an old saying, "Snake in the Chung Mountains." When the snake in the Chung Mountains is struck at its head, it will counter with its tail, and if the tail is struck, it will counter with its head. It seems to be an imaginary creature, like the mythical snake, *tsuchinoko*. Likewise, Japan should not be such a fragile country that will be crushed as soon as a part of it is attacked. Japan needs to have several regions that can make important decisions and protect its pride as a sovereign nation.

4

Your Faith in God or Buddha Will Help You Make the Right Decisions

Remove your false self and avoid falling to hell

To sum up what I want to tell you today, one of the ways to avoid falling to hell is to remove your false self and face your true self. I want you to think about how you can do so based on our teachings. This is the first point.

Conceit is not a problem that only applies to people with tengu-like, conceited tendencies. When people are young, they want to grow and develop themselves, which is a natural feeling as a human being. Everyone, including animals, loves themselves. Animals love themselves more than anything else. That is why they strive to live, grow, and survive even if it means eating other creatures. Human beings also have this tendency. The desire for self-growth and self-development, the desire to be an important person, and the desire to succeed in this world are endless. When these desires are manifested on a national scale, a small country would want to grow bigger, an overpopulated country would want to take over another country, and a country with increased military power would want to take over other countries.

However, once you become top-level, whether as a country or as a person, you must not think about yourself only. Please know that if all you can think about is how you can benefit yourself, you cannot be top-level in the truest sense.

Freedom should be granted to those who can discipline themselves

I do not intend to say anything difficult. But if you want to become a top-level person, let me mention one thing you need to check yourself against.

I, too, like and enjoy freedom. I want to do things freely, I want to let others do things freely, and I want to create a society with freedom. However, freedom does not mean letting things be unleashed. Freedom should be granted only to those who can control and discipline themselves.

For example, if you happen to find a stash of money right in front of you, you must be able to tell whether this money is something you are allowed to spend or not. If you are working in a company, you must be able to tell whether the company's money is something you can spend or not. If you are on a date with someone and it gets late at night, you must know when it is time for you to go home. People who can control themselves in these situations will be able to develop themselves further with freedom, but those who cannot will, although it may not sound very pleasant, often be "bound" by others. In other words, they will often need to be disciplined from the outside.

However, if this discipline or restriction applied in society goes too far, the society will become no different from an authoritarian country. Its citizens will be regarded as ignorant fools, put under the same rules, and treated as if they are cockroaches. In this kind of country, only the leaders are regarded as smart and the rest are regarded as people who cannot think. So, in a sense, intellectuals need to work harder to change the situation in these countries.

The key point is self-discipline. In a parent-child relationship, a child often seeks freedom from his or her parents, saying, "I want to achieve my dream. Let me do what I want to do." This struggle can also be seen among siblings, and also in a company. People want to do things freely in their own way. If you are the kind of person who has control over yourself, having freedom is important and is a good thing for you. For example, if you are entrusted with freedom at work, it means people around you are confident that you will always consider the best interest of the company and make decisions based on it, even when others are not watching. However, if others are afraid of what you would do when you are given freedom, you will not get it. The same is true with family members. Just because the person is your sibling, eldest son or daughter, or only child, does not necessarily mean you can entrust them with everything.

In this way, when you assess a person, you must see whether he or she is a self-disciplined person. This also applies to yourself. A self-disciplined person has the right to seek more freedom. But if the person is a kind who cannot be trusted unless they are under supervision, or if you think you are this type of person, such people must live within the boundaries of the rules, such as school rules, company rules, or precepts of a religious group. Otherwise, the person will most likely make mistakes.

If people were allowed to drive as they like on highways, there would certainly be many accidents. So, rules have to be set. Some people who do not make mistakes even without rules may think they are different from the conceited, tengu-type people, but mistakes can happen to everyone.

Laws and political decisions should be made based on faith

This problem can be seen in a dictatorship as well. Its leader can make many people follow him because, in a way, he has strong leadership. But we need to look carefully at whether he is capable of disciplining himself. This is a point to check. Is he someone with strong desires who tries to realize them even at the cost of suppressing others? This is the point you must examine.

Former U.S. President Trump was criticized a lot by the media, but when he was president, he only received one dollar a year. He probably had no intention of making money as a politician. He only received a dollar, but only a few Japanese people probably know about this and very few media report it. He served as president with a one-dollar salary. He appears to be a trickster with a sharp tongue, so he is easily misunderstood, but he does not seem to have much selfish motive and he is straightforward. That is why he can be trusted.

Speaking of being straightforward and credible, I feel that recently, there are not many lies in what Mr. Kim Jong-un and Mr. Xi Jinping say. They probably mean what they say, so in a sense, they may be somewhat credible. Rather, I feel more skeptical toward democracy. Sometimes, leaders of democratic countries have to lie to stay in power, so they lie a lot. Yet, when they honestly admit their mistakes, they are fired straightaway. I think this is a bad aspect of democracy. Honest people are fired easily, whereas those who lie to get away with problems stay in power longer. The administration that lies often is in power for longer and politicians of this type also stay longer in ministerial posts. This is a paradox in democracy.

In fact, only about one-third or a little over 30 percent of the countries in the world are democratic. Even so, Mr. Biden says, "We must defend democracy," and upholds this slogan as a good cause. But I would like to say that only less than half of the countries in the world are democratic. Many countries are yet to be modernized and their people are seeking powerful leaders. That is why they sometimes elect a president who, in the eyes of the people of foreign nations, is not worthy to be a leader. This shows that many countries are still not very developed.

Democracy works only in a society where the majority of people can be entrusted with freedom or can make sound decisions when they gain the freedom to participate in politics. What is important here is people's faith in God or Buddha. This is what it all stems from. The laws are mere rules that humans have worked together to make, so they are not almighty. What people need is faith in God or Buddha, the Being who stands above humans. Only then can people establish the right laws, make the right political decisions, and take the right actions.

My opinion on the shooting incident of the former prime minister of Japan

In the summer of 2022, a former Japanese prime minister was shot and killed during his campaign speech.

Apparently, the killer was upset when he learned that his mother donated almost all of the family's savings to a religious group over a suicide in the family. So, he shot the prime minister (who had received support from the religious group) with a homemade gun. But the case is now developing in an incomprehensible way. Usually, the killer should be the one condemned, but instead, the religious group that the killer was against is being oppressed and is almost driven into dissolution. Amid all this, other religious groups have been caught in the crossfire and things are turning out quite strange.

It is also strange that the ones who received support are now oppressing the ones who gave them support. If the Liberal Democratic Party goes on like this, no one would want to support them anymore.

Currently, the Japanese government has a budget deficit, so they may want to impose all kinds of taxes on religious organizations, including shrines and temples, and collect a lot of money. Shrines such as Meiji Jingu and Ise Jingu have large areas of land, so the government would be able to make money if a property tax were imposed on them.

Not only that, the government could also try to take money from their members. If the members donated their assets to religion upon death, the government would not be happy. So they might think of ways to get that money via tax, for example. I presume that a battle to seize the assets of deceased people will begin in the near future. Nowadays, when an incident happens, rather than addressing the actual problem, many people try to take advantage of it and benefit themselves. So, we need to be wary.

As for us, we keep voicing our opinions about political matters, and even speaking up on things that other political candidates hesitate to say out of fear of losing in elections. We place more importance on sticking to what is right. In terms of our political movement, we are yet to become full-fledged; out of about 2,000 staff members at Happy Science, only about 50 of them are assigned to our political wing, the Happiness Realization Party. Our party is carrying out activities on a small scale with only about 50 staff members, so it may look small. Luckily, since we are not yet a "big shot," we are still able to carry out activities comfortably without being bound by the rules put under the idea of separation of religion and state. But I believe society will eventually change, so we would like to continue making efforts in our political activities.

In our case, we also have believers in parties other than the Happiness Realization Party. We have believers among the lawmakers of the Liberal Democratic Party, the Constitutional Democratic Party, the National Democratic Party, and sometimes even the Komeito Party and the Communist Party. Regarding our political stance, we accept supporters from different political groups. You may not believe it, but people from other political parties indeed support us. I, too, am surprised. There is even a lawmaker of the Communist Party who has been a Happy Science member for several decades. He admires the theoretical part of our teachings. In fact, the Communist Party is very logical and its members like logical ideas. That is why, when they see us criticizing the administration straight to the point, many of them find it appealing and become our believers. When we criticize the administration, we do it straightforwardly, so some Communist Party members are moved and tell us, "I always read your politics-related books." We have believers in the Komeito Party (a political party of another religious group) as well.

In the past, when there were more parties than there are now, we had many believers who were lawmakers, including party leaders. We had many members even among the former ministers who belonged to the Liberal Democratic Party. None of them are in office anymore, so we do not have to worry about being accused of having connections to politicians. I feel relieved about that. However, essentially, there is nothing wrong with religions supporting political activities. What is important is that we must always bear in mind to consider whether something is true or false, or right or wrong.

The coronavirus warfare is a prelude to nuclear war

Since a person from the *Tokushima Shimbun Newspaper* is here to listen to my lecture today, I was advised not to mention this because I might offend him. But then again, I must say that when I read their editorial this morning that said, "It is better to prevent academic research and civilian technology from being diverted to military use," I thought, "Why would they write this now?" They write such an editorial at a time when a ballistic missile lands near Hokkaido. I, myself, want to say at least Hokkaido University should consider doing the research because it landed near them. I know that it is currently forbidden to conduct this kind of research at national universities. But as I told the former Minister of Education, Culture, Sports, Science and Technology long ago, Japan should conduct research on this matter to protect the lives of its people.

As for the coronavirus, I have been saying from the beginning that this is an experiment of biological warfare that is happening before a nuclear war begins. This was my view from the outset. In reality, more than 600 million people have been infected and about a million people have died (at the time of the lecture). To put it bluntly, this death toll is at the level of a world war. And I think this is just a prelude. We will see how it goes from now on.

It is difficult to tell who the culprit is if bacteria or viruses are used as a weapon. It is a "nuclear weapon of the poor," which means that even a small country can use it.

That is why I thought a war had begun when the pandemic broke out. It has been about three years since then, but I do not think that it is over yet. We will need another two years or so before things go back to how they were, so we still have a few more years to bear.

But what comes after this is the crisis of a nuclear war. That is what will be nearing from next year onwards, so we must brace ourselves. It is too optimistic to think that an atomic bomb will never be used again just because Japan suffered it once. Rather, it is precisely because Japan suffered it that we must speak up and tell the world what would happen if an atomic bomb were to be dropped. Even if Ukraine were to be under nuclear attack, people in other countries would not suffer because it is not their problem. Perhaps they may feel sorry for the people of Ukraine, but that will be all.

The U.S. is the only evenly matched country that can fight a nuclear war with Russia now, but observing Mr. Biden's military strategy, it is obvious that his basic policy is to lend conventional weapons but avoid any troubles concerning nuclear wars. This means that what is happening in Ukraine will also happen in the Korean Peninsula, Taiwan, and Japan. The U.S. will lend us conventional weapons but will not fight a nuclear war for us. We need to know this. I hope Japan will make further advancements in science and technology and acquire the technology needed to protect its people.

The important points to keep in mind as an individual and as a country

Today's lecture is for the commemoration of the First Turning of the Wheel of Truth, so it is more like an introductory talk. In the next two public lectures, I intend to state more clearly the direction Japan must take next year (refer to Chapters Two and Three).

As an individual, first, remove your false ego or false self and make an effort to develop an honest mind. When the desire to make oneself look bigger and stronger manifests on a national level, such nations may develop the tendency to occupy and rule over other countries. So, we need to observe the leaders of authoritarian countries carefully and see through their minds.

In addition, we should not look at other countries with overly good intentions. There is a red line we must keep. A country that shoots missiles so frequently, almost every day, has lost its mind, so we need to deal with it appropriately. In such cases, we must put its leaders in straitjackets and take them away under guard, just as how a mental hospital treats its patients. This is how serious the situation is currently looking. We must be strong when we need to be, and kind when we need to be. It is important to have both attributes and use them accordingly as we live.

Today, I talked a little about political matters as well. We will continue to speak out fairly and impartially, and we intend to support all those who are working to make Japan better. The Happiness Realization Party has been going through an "honorable defeat." When we see that other parties do not speak up, we come up and say what needs to be said and often end up losing the election. That is fine for now, though. I do not mind because we are carrying out religious activities as well. We will keep on working hard so that our group will eventually become a compass that can guide the way for the world.

We still have a long way to go. The fight will continue. Let us work together so that our country will not perish while you are alive.

CHAPTER TWO

Making the Way to True Salvation

Originally recorded in Japanese on December 6, 2022
at Saitama Super Arena in Saitama, Japan
and later translated into English.

1

The Majority Vote Cannot Determine Whether Religion Is Right or Wrong

The reason that this lecture is titled, "Making the Way to True Salvation"

The theme of today's lecture is, "Making the Way to True Salvation." The reason is ever since this summer (2022), there has been a lot of debate in Japan over how religion should be and how to determine whether a particular religion is right or wrong. Happy Science is one of the leading religions in Japan, so I am sure many people want to hear our thoughts on this issue too.

There are 180,000 religious groups in Japan, but even I do not know them all, so I cannot comment on each one of them. Neither do I know the many religious groups in the world and what they are all doing.

Put simply, another way of saying "True Salvation" is "Please join Happy Science," and that would be it. But I humbly think that people may not agree with this with the amount of effort and achievement we have made so far. Christians can get by with it; all they need to say is, "If you become a Christian, you will be saved." [*Laughs.*]

Having said that, the title of today's lecture, "Making the Way to True Salvation," is a translation of the original Japanese title (*Shukyo no Hondo wo Ayumu*). When I saw it, I thought that the meaning of it was slightly off from my Japanese title. The impression that the English title gives is, "Join Happy Science, and you will surely be saved," and it is very Christian-like. But in reality, the efforts we have made are far from enough to be able to say that. We are still not at the level where all I need to talk about is Happy Science and state that it is the only way to true salvation.

So today, I will, as much as I can, try to talk about things that are close to today's theme. At the same time, I will summarize what we have done as a religion over the last 36 years (at the time of the lecture) from my standpoint, and share my current feelings and thoughts based on it.

How the Japanese mass media and legal system are reacting to a religious group in question

To start off, I must say that a public opinion poll cannot determine whether a religion is right or wrong, or give an answer to the question, "What is true salvation?" I would like you to remember this.

Essentially, the work of a religion is to establish order, pave the way, and indicate the direction to a large crowd of people who are lost in ignorance. So, collecting various people's opinions and analyzing them saying, "This is right," "This is mainstream," or "This is the majority," will not lead us to the right answer. In a way, the principles that underlie religion are completely different from those of modern academic learning, politics, or science.

In the world of religion, it is possible for only one person to be in the right. And it may take 500, 1,000, or even 2,000 years until people realize that what he or she said was truly right. So, I do not think that what is right will be completely justified, understood, or accepted in the same time period as it is being taught or carried out. In reality, a new religion always emerges out of necessity because the common sense or majority opinion of the given time is mistaken. That is why, historically, new religions have often been suppressed and persecuted. In some cases, they have been re-evaluated in later generations and were acknowledged as righteous, while many others disappeared from history.

Historically, numerous light of archangels and angels—or in the Japanese context, *dai-nyorai* (great tathagatas), *nyorai* (tathagatas), and *bosatsu* (bodhisattvas)—have descended on earth. But unfortunately, many of them were defeated, persecuted, suppressed, or eliminated one after another. Opposing forces triumphed over them many times. This is the truth seen from the heavenly world.

At this current point in time, it is very difficult to tell what is right and what is wrong. However, what is clear is that a statistical approach, such as a majority vote, cannot be used to decide what is right. The only way to get close to it is to keep observing with a pure mind whether the Truth being taught is really true, whether the love being taught is really true, and whether the mind being taught is really sacred.

Since this summer, the Japanese media has been criticizing a lot about a particular religion that is spreading, not only in Japan but also overseas. So religion, as a whole, is put in a difficult situation. At present, discussions seem to be underway in the Japanese Diet about setting a legal cap on offerings. But frankly speaking, these discussions are completely irrelevant to religion. Religious offerings are different from political funds that have regulations. They are not the same. So, it is absolutely ridiculous to bring up the concept of consumer contracts in religion. It has nothing to do with religion. Religion is not a consumer industry, nor is it a contract. If the word "contract" were to be used in religion, the contract would be between God and humans, but there is not a single human being in this world who is at the level to make a contract with God. Therefore, the basic attitude that humans should take is to accept and follow God's teachings.

It is easy for us to conclude that the religious group, which has been an issue since the summer in Japan, is an evil religion, and we have many reasons for this. But generally speaking, if the tables are turned, people will see things differently. People are granted freedom of speech, publication, religion, and academic learning based on the belief that humans are good-natured. It is under a belief that through free competition, what is right will surely be established and what is wrong will naturally be weeded out. This belief is a part of the Constitution of Japan and also the Western values of the world. Therefore, we should not determine whether a religion is right or wrong based on surveys conducted by the mass media. Instead, people of various religious groups must speak out their opinions and have the public decide on what they think is right or wrong.

2

The Truth Taught by Sages Is Rarely Accepted During Their Lifetime

Confucius and Socrates
were rejected by the people

Unfortunately, as you can see from history, almost all of the Four Great Sages were not even fully accepted by the people during their lifetime. They are Shakyamuni Buddha, Jesus Christ, Socrates, and Confucius.

Confucius served as a minister of justice or public works for a short period in his home country. It was for about one year. After that, he wandered different countries looking for work as a government official, but could not find any post to become a minister. It was only his teachings that became widely used by later generations. Confucius of course had a group of disciples, and I am guessing he taught around 3,000 people. I hesitate to say this, but his group was probably smaller than the Happiness Realization Party. This political party founded by Happy Science has many more supporters.

There is also Socrates. He gave a brilliant and eloquent defense known as the "Apology of Socrates." It has been passed down throughout history and is still read today. Socrates was given an opportunity to defend himself after he was judged evil. Despite giving a magnificent speech, even more people voted for the death penalty after the speech. This was truly regrettable. People made a wrong judgment, which is the shame of humanity. It is recorded in the *Apology of Socrates* and has been read for 2,500 years. Even so, humans have not yet repented of it. It has only been handed down as a mere incident that happened long ago because people cannot relate to how people felt back then.

Socrates was charged with not believing in Greek gods and misleading the Greek youth. He was declared guilty in both cases. He was accused of teaching about a non-Greek god. In Greece, Zeus was the main god, and people said that Socrates' teachings were different from those of Zeus. But this is a matter of course. Although Zeus was regarded as a god and was called the omniscient and omnipotent, what he did was fool around with women. If he were living today, weekly gossip magazines would be full of articles of him questioning whether he has done any good. You could say that Zeus was very similar to the Tokugawa warlords who were striving to make children, as often depicted in the historical dramas on NHK (Japan Broadcasting Corporation). Other than that, there is nothing about him worth mentioning in particular. People admired him only because he was said to be a god.

Jewish people could not understand that Jesus was a messiah

Then, there is Jesus. Jesus was crucified on the hill of Golgotha. A church now stands there, so you cannot see the exact site of his crucifixion. But there, he was stabbed in the side with a spear, had his legs broken so that he could die quickly, and was buried. That was his life on earth.

I sometimes try to imagine what he went through. I am sure it was painful. In my case, I will try to work to the age that I plan to live to, and then depart for the other world. What the Jewish people did to Jesus was a shame of humanity. It was way beyond shameful, and it was the worst thing humans could do. It was the worst of the worst, and the most evil.

It is a mystery as to why the Jewish race still survives to this day. But this is because Jesus was Jewish. In other words, it would mean that if you denounce Jesus, you can denounce the Jewish people, but because you cannot denounce Jesus, you cannot denounce the Jewish people. Jesus thought of himself as Jewish. He lived his life, gave teachings, and died believing that he was a Jewish messiah. However, even the people with strong faith who lived in the same age as Jesus could not see him as such.

Shakyamuni Buddha chose to preach the teachings over protecting the Shakya Kingdom

Shakyamuni Buddha was relatively successful in this world among the Four Great Sages. It is true that he was persecuted a couple of times, but he continued to preach his teachings and lived long until the age of 80, which is considered equivalent to the age of 120 in modern times. He lived very long and continued to give teachings. Even the teachings he gave in his very last moments remain to this day. In this sense, he lived a successful and happy life.

Gautama Siddhartha, or Shakyamuni Buddha, left Kapilavastu, abandoned his status as a prince, and underwent, not three, but six years of spiritual discipline before he finally conquered the devil and became a buddha. He then formed a group of disciples and his teachings spread widely. However, after Shakyamuni left his parents and renounced the world, his father died, and the Shakya clan was destroyed. Only 500 people from the Shakya clan who became his followers survived. The Shakya Kingdom, which was a vassal state to Kosala, was destroyed and those who remained in the castle were all killed, although I believe some of them had managed to escape. In Nepal, there are Happy Science believers named Shakya, so they are most likely the descendants of the Shakya clan. This shows that some must have survived, but in any case, the Shakya clan is believed to have been annihilated.

Although Shakyamuni Buddha's stepmother, wife, son, and some young men renounced the world and became monks and nuns, the kingdom itself perished while Buddha was still alive. Also, when Buddha was around 72 years old, one of his disciples, Devadatta, revolted against him. It was a tragic time, and I think it was around this time when the Shakya Kingdom perished. It perished in Shakyamuni Buddha's later years, some years before he died at 80. This was the tremendous price he paid. He must have grieved deeply.

Nonetheless, we do not know whether the kingdom could have survived had Shakyamuni Buddha succeeded the king. There were 16 other kingdoms that were stronger than the Shakya Kingdom, so it could have been destroyed regardless. Nothing in this world remains forever. The incidents show that something that was thought to remain forever perished fleetingly in this transient world. Although Shakyamuni Buddha, himself, was able to leave behind a good amount of teachings by continuously preaching for 45 years, his kingdom perished because he did not succeed the king.

In this way, all of the Four Great Sages experienced sadness—they all experienced "the impermanence of all things" and "the egolessness of all phenomena." In this way, whether what a person teaches is the Truth or not can hardly be judged based on the person's success or failure in this world.

Saviors such as Mani and Hong Xiuquan were disregarded on earth

Many people whom we recognize as saviors sent from the heavenly world disappeared without being accepted by the people of this world. It is disappointing. It is really sad.

One of them was Mani, who was active about 100 or 200 years after the establishment of Christianity. His teachings spread widely and became a world religion in his time. But while he was alive, he was attacked by Zoroastrian followers and was sentenced to death by being flayed. Aurelius Augustinus (St. Augustine) once believed in the teachings of Mani, but later repented for having believed in an "evil religion" and wrote it in his book, *Confessions*. This book is still being read today.

However, Manichaeism was not an evil religion. When the high spirits in heaven thought Christianity had failed after Jesus' crucifixion, they sent Mani down. But 200 to 300 years after Christianity seemed to have failed, it regained power and grew bigger than Manichaeism. What is surprising is Zoroastrianism is actually a religion that is said to have been started by Mani himself in his past life. So he was executed by the very religion he had founded in his previous life. Such an unthinkable thing actually happened.

Another example is Hong Xiuquan in China. He was sent from heaven as a messiah or savior in the 1800s and led the Taiping Rebellion to stage a revolution against the declining Qing dynasty. But the Qing dynasty, which would lose in a war against Japan (First Sino-Japanese War in the late 1800s), had stood strong against religion. About 50 million followers of Hong Xiuquan are said to have been killed in the rebellion, which is a huge number of people. In a sense, I feel Taiwan, South Korea, and Japan might face something similar to this in the near future.

Therefore, I want you to understand that, generally, even a savior's teachings are not fully accepted by people who are living in the same age as him. Even so, what is important is to consider whether you can find, in what is being taught, something that truly speaks to your soul. Religions that teach the Truth may not be accepted in a worldly sense on certain occasions and instead be attacked, criticized, or rejected because many people do not think well of religion on the whole. In Japan, a couple of religious groups were labeled as evil religions and forced to dissolve, so about 20 to 30 percent of the

Japanese people are probably thinking, "After we're done with the Unification Church, let's attack Soka Gakkai and Happy Science next!" Well, it is OK for them to think this way, but we will try our best not to lose. We have no intention of losing to them.

3

As a World Religion, Happy Science Will Continue to Speak Out on What Is Right

The importance of national defense

Especially regarding national defense, only 13 percent of Japanese people think that Japan should defend itself. This is the worst percentage in the world. Happy Science is a religion that speaks out about politics including national defense, but I assume many people think this act, in itself, is wrong and that religion should not speak about politics in the first place. I am fully aware of such arguments.

But I would like you to look back at what I have been teaching in the last 30 years. The things I have been saying were indeed mostly correct. Many things have turned out the way I said they would. The people in Happy Science understand this, but unfortunately, there are only a very few people outside of Happy Science who would analyze what I have said in the last 30 years and admit that things have truly turned out the way I said they would.

In the recent newspaper, it said, that since North Korea has been launching missiles one after another and developing nuclear weapons, the Japanese government has now finally decided to buy 500 Tomahawk cruise missiles from the U.S. in five years' time. Five hundred missiles in five years—hopefully, things won't be too late by then. The point is, what if North Korea makes a move in the fourth year? What if they do something in the second year? I have been warning Japan for the last 30 years about this, but the government did not listen. So all I will just say is, "I hope five years later won't be too late."

The Japanese government is saying that Japan will also develop long-range missiles domestically so it can at least defend itself. I am not sure whom these comments are addressed to. Just imagining that the ruling party members are 30 years behind Happy Science makes me dizzy but... Wait, no, we must not be conceited. We should not think we are smarter than them [*laughs*]; thinking such things will only invite oppression. I am sure they are all "intelligent people." They probably all believe that nothing bad will happen in life or in the world. They are just happy as long as they can live through each day. They are happy-go-lucky people. As long as they can just watch the World Cup and have enough to eat every day, they are happy. I don't mean to make them feel bad though [*audience laughs*].

My thoughts on World Cup Soccer
—Japan vs. Croatia

Earlier today, at midnight, there was the World Cup game between Japan and Croatia. It was tempting to watch, wasn't it? Many of you may have thought last night, "Since Master's lecture starts at 7 p.m. tomorrow, it shouldn't be too much of a problem if I watch a 90-minute game at midnight. I could snooze a little during work before going to the lecture. I could try to leave work early by saying, 'I am feeling under the weather.' Then, I can make it in time for the lecture." It is indeed hard to resist the temptation.

As for me, I told myself last night, "I mustn't be tempted. I must get to bed before midnight because I have to work tomorrow." But I could not sleep until around 1 a.m., so I ended up turning on the TV and watching the game [*laughs*]. So, I am afraid I am in no position to scold you. Since I could not sleep anyway, I thought it would be OK to watch the game, which I ended up doing. I just watched it thinking that it's only another 45 minutes. But that wasn't the case. It was supposed to be a 90-minute game, but they added an extra 30 minutes. I thought, "Another 30 minutes! Oh, no. What if it affects my condition tomorrow?" But the game still did not end after the additional 30 minutes, and then came the penalty shootout. I thought, "What!? Unbelievable! It will be daybreak soon. When is this game going to end? What if I start dozing off in front of everyone and ruin the lecture because of this? I am supposed to be telling everyone not to watch soccer but to focus on religion. This is not good." Although I had such thoughts, I could not resist watching the game.

I knew this was wrong as a religious leader, so I then decided to watch it in bed [*audience laughs*]. I lay down on my side and covered myself with a blanket. I was watching the game half asleep and opened my eyes to important moments. I did not expect the game to last that long. It did not last until dawn. The game ended around 3 a.m., which meant there was not much time to sleep. Anyway, this is how I ended up watching the soccer game for two hours and then the shootout as well.

I cannot pick a side
—there are believers in both Japan and Croatia

While watching the shootout, I realized that Croatia was strong. I did not know that until then. The teams were evenly matched, and I thought perhaps Japan could score one more goal. But the Croatian players were big. They were all very well-built, which made me wonder what they were eating. Maybe they have huge cows in Croatia. I thought about these things as I watched the game. They were tall, well-built and had much longer legs than the Japanese players. When they had the ball, they controlled it with incredible skills. Although the Croatian team looked quite strong, the game ended in a tie, so I thought the two teams, Croatia and Japan, were about the same level.

However, during the shootout, it became clear that the Croatian players were much stronger. There was a huge difference in their levels. Japanese players kept on kicking "grounders," but Croatian players kicked the ball in the air and were shooting accurately. Croatia won 3 to 1 in the shootout, but considering the difference in level between the two teams, it would not have been strange if Japan lost 1 to 3 in the match itself. So, I thought, after all, Japan did great to end the match in a tie. While I was congratulating the Japanese team on their effort, I was also congratulating the Happy Science members in Croatia for their victory, as we have believers in Croatia, too. This is what it means to be a world religion. You cannot just cheer for one side. There are Happy Science members in Croatia too, so I cannot just support one side. I am happy for Croatia as well.

Being a soccer player is the most popular career in Croatia, so I was happy for them to have been recognized by the world. I also wondered what they eat to build their bodies. With a body like theirs, I think that they would defeat Japan for sure in a physical fight, too. These things often happen when I am caught between two things. Happy Science aims to be a world religion, but the more worldwide Happy Science becomes, the more restricted I will be with what I can say.

What could have been done to prevent the Russo-Ukrainian War?

For example, the Russo-Ukrainian War has started. Those two countries are now in a war. This lecture is also being broadcast at the Happy Science branch in Russia, though our members there may watch it later because of the time difference. So, I cannot openly criticize Russia. I can say things indirectly, but not officially because it can upset our members in Russia.

But we also have Happy Science members in Ukraine which, according to the global opinion or the Western opinion, is being "invaded" by Russia. So, I am thinking, "Will the Ukrainian members be OK? What should I do? Will they leave Happy Science? If I speak too well of Russia, will they be troubled?" We have many members in the EU as well. Our members are everywhere, so if I start thinking about supporting every country, I will not be able to say anything. In a conflict, there will always be followers of our teachings on both sides.

Currently, Ukraine is receiving weapons mainly from the U.K. and France to gain an advantage in the war.

However, it is difficult to judge whether this move is right or not.

I have been giving quite harsh opinions on this matter. What I say is different from the mainstream media. I believe this Russo-Ukrainian War was unnecessary. There was no need for it. So then, what should have been done in the first place? The answer is, if Ukraine had declared to take a neutral position, a war would not have happened. It is as simple as that. I understand that the Ukrainian president wants to join the EU and try to fight against Russia by using NATO forces. But it was obvious from the outset that Russia would not keep silent about that. This war would not have started had Ukraine maintained its neutral stance. It was Mr. Biden's strategy to use Ukraine—which is neither a part of the EU nor NATO—and start a skirmish against Russia by offering weapons to Ukraine. He probably expected that by helping Ukraine, the U.S. would be able to recover economically without suffering any damage.

What will happen if the Russo-Ukrainian War is drawn out?

Japanese people, including most of the mass media and scholars, think that the world understands how terrible nuclear weapons are based on the dropping of two atomic bombs, one in Hiroshima and the other in Nagasaki, during World War II. They blindly believe that no country will ever use such inhumane weapons again.

But in reality, many countries are developing nuclear weapons, and of course, not for the purpose of possessing them without using them. They are developing these weapons so that they can use them when the need arises. Or perhaps, they possess nuclear weapons as a form of threat to other countries and imply that such weapons will be used if they cannot win with conventional weapons. So, the Japanese common sense is indeed nonsense to the rest of the world.

So far, Russia has not used nuclear weapons. However, if the U.S., U.K., and France continue to supply weapons to Ukraine and draw out the war, and if the tide turns unfavorable for Russia and puts them on the verge of surrender in a battle of conventional weapons, then Russia might really resort to using nuclear weapons. We should all know that this is a real possibility. Therefore, it is wrong to assume that supporting Ukraine will help them win. Instead, it could bring about the worst-case scenario.

Another issue is that Kiev, which is now called Kyiv, is the Holy Land of the Russian Orthodox Church. It is "Jerusalem" for Russia. The Russian Orthodox Church started there. For Russia, Kiev is a place that they must protect and keep under control. If Kiev establishes independence or joins the EU, there may be an endless Crusades-like war. Also, when Mikhail Gorbachev was the president of the Soviet Union, he owned a second home in Ukraine and often visited there on vacation. So, you need to know that for Russia, Ukraine is not just another foreign country.

I will say no more on this matter because if I do, it could cause all kinds of trouble. It seems that many people believe that the EU is stronger than Russia in a conventional war. But in terms of nuclear weapons, the U.K. and France only have about 300 each whereas Russia has 6,000 to 7,000. So, the EU will lose if they fight against Russia in an all-out war. People should know this.

Japanese people blindly believe that nuclear weapons will never be used and that no country would dare to use them. Similarly, the people in Ukraine may believe the same and think that repeatedly reciting this "belief" like a mantra will bring them victory. But in an all-out war, Russia will ultimately win.

The U.S. is the only country that can fight on par with Russia. Sadly, I can only perceive Mr. Biden as a two-headed alien. To me, he looks like an alien with two Godzilla-like heads, but I will not reveal the secret behind this. I won't. Since many people are listening to this lecture in dozens of places in the U.S. as well, I will not say it.

What is more, my political opinions are often similar to those of the Republican Party. But since there are more Democrats than Republicans among our American members, it is not easy for me to express my opinions. I supported Mr. Trump in the election before the previous one, but the majority of Happy Science members in the U.S. were supporters of the Democratic Party. Indeed, it is very difficult to make religion and politics work together harmoniously. The Democratic Party says a lot about human rights, so religious people tend to become their supporters. There are many Hollywood stars that I like, but a good number of them also support the Democratic Party. I have mixed feelings on this; I remain a fan of the actors, but at the same time, in terms of politics, I am clearly stating that their opinions are wrong and showing the right direction. So I, too, am in a difficult position.

How would the world have turned out if Mr. Trump had won the 2020 U.S. presidential election?

How would things have turned out if Mr. Trump had won the presidential election in 2020? It is true that he won a historical number of votes as a Republican candidate, so let us simulate what would have happened if he had been the U.S. president. First of all, North Korea would not have launched missiles this often or developed nuclear weapons to its current level. I am certain about this. Mr. Trump was doing a good job. In his talks with North Korea, he said to Kim Jong-un, "Let's not fight anymore. A nuclear war will not bring you a better future. Look at Vietnam. It used to be a communist country but saw development after adopting the market-based economy.

Why don't you become like Vietnam?" Kim Jong-un was actually expecting that things might work out well if Mr. Trump was the one he talked to.

The recent missile launches by North Korea are a crisis for Japan in terms of national defense, but their missiles were mainly launched during the period before the U.S. midterm elections. They stopped firing missiles after that because they did not want to waste them. The fact that they shot missiles only before the midterm elections means that these were "fireworks" to express their support for Republicans. They were sending the message, "We want Mr. Trump back as the U.S. president" because they believed they could make negotiations with Mr. Trump.

But I believe Mr. Biden would not even visit North Korea because he is scared. He is cowardly, so he will never cross the 38th parallel and step into North Korea. He probably will not meet Mr. Putin, either. He is scared; he is old and quite timid. Even so, he wants to make himself look good. From this, we can say that Mr. Trump is a brave man.

Japan is now saying that they will buy 500 Tomahawk cruise missiles and also develop long-range missiles themselves. I do not know if the missiles will come in time while Japan still needs them, or if it will just be a waste of money. But in any case, if Mr. Trump was the president, Japan may not need missiles because he would probably have tried to change North Korea into a country like Vietnam.

The same is true in terms of Ukraine. Mr. Putin and Mr. Trump were getting along well, so the problem between Ukraine and Russia, too, might well have been resolved over a phone call. If, before the Russo-Ukrainian War, Mr. Trump had said that he would talk with Mr. Putin in person, the war may have never happened. However, now, we do not know how many people have been killed in this war because neither Russia nor Ukraine revealed the real death tolls. It will be a big problem if this war drags on. The president of Ukraine, in particular, knows very well how to make himself look good on TV. It seems he is trying to make Ukraine look like one of the democratic nations by joining NATO and the EU, but Ukraine is by no means a democratic nation. It is now a completely dictatorial nation. Ukrainian adult men cannot leave the country, and they are told to fight to death. This is similar to how the Japanese military carried things out toward the end of World War II.

Try to understand my opinions deeply because I can foresee the future

As you can see from the above, the reality can often end up quite the opposite of what the mainstream mass media reports. The media may support one side based on the ideology it upholds to this day, but ironically, the reality could head in the opposite direction.

In most cases, you cannot judge one side to be 100 percent right and the other to be 100 percent wrong. Nonetheless, as you can see from what I have been saying in the last 30 years, I can foresee the future to some extent. Please know this. I may not be 100 percent accurate, but I rarely ever misread the trend of the times. So, please try to understand deeply what Ryuho Okawa is saying when considering things.

As I have believers on both sides of the countries in conflict, I feel torn when I have to send a message to support either side. Even so, I sometimes dare to state my opinions. So, please understand the situation I am in and try to accept my words by thinking, "He may have a point because he dares to speak out despite his difficult position."

Had Mr. Trump continued to serve as the president, our only issue would have been China. Speaking of China, we, Happy Science, have been fighting hard against them. In my song, "Farewell, Xiang Xiang," there is a line that says, "Xiang Xiang, if you don't like totalitarianism, if you find that the Chinese bamboo is not to your taste, or if you aren't pleased with your arranged husband, you can come back here (to Japan) at any time." This is, in fact, a kind of resistance movement. We wish Xiang Xiang did not have to go back to China. She is very pretty for a panda. She is adorable. She has showmanship. She has the power to improve the economy. She could gather four million visitors with her adorable performance. She is more charming than the average singer or actor. It is a shame we have to send her back. Ueno Zoo will surely be quieter with fewer visitors. I cannot help but think of such thoughts. Well, I should not just talk about Xiang Xiang alone. Pandas live in several different countries, so it is unclear if they belong to a specific country. Pandas were already in existence five million years ago and their fossils were found in Spain, as well. Our spiritual readings have also revealed the truth that pandas have a much older history.

4

To Make the Way to True Salvation

The main work of religion that must not be left out

Going back to the topic, "Making the Way to True Salvation," there is one point that I must not leave out. What is it?

Now, the world is becoming more convenient to live in. Science is advancing and a lot of useful things have been developed in terms of economy and politics. Japan is also heading in this direction. I think the majority of people favor the fact that the world is making advancements. It is good when things become more convenient. However, when this world becomes too convenient, people tend to disregard the other world. Scientism and materialism will lead us to a world like this.

We recently published the book, *The Laws of Hell*. It is the Laws Series for next year (2023) and will be our main book for the year. I would like you to know that hell still exists even in this modern age when science has made advancements, when rockets are being launched and we see bullet trains running here and there. Heaven also still exists.

Indeed, medical science has advanced. Smart people are going on to study medicine and are working hard to cure illnesses and extend the human lifespan. The average life expectancy has increased since World War II, which means smart people have succeeded in their jobs.

However, you must remember that not a single person can live forever. A person may extend their life by 10 to 20 years, but it is 100 percent certain that everyone will die one day. Some people believe that their life in this world is all there is and they are happy as long as they can enjoy the convenience and pleasure in this world. Others believe that life continues after death and think about how they should live in this world. It is upon death that the difference between these two types of people will become clear.

If you just look at the efforts and achievements you have made in this world, you will see that the efforts you put in are not always rewarded. In this world, a cause does not always bring about an effect. However, when you look at the bigger picture, or if you include the other world, a cause will always bring an effect; it is a complete cycle. That is how God created the world.

People nowadays live longer. Regardless, the other world still exists. Although Christianity does not teach this enough, the fact is that we have souls and have led spiritual lives before we were born on earth. I have taught these things in *The Laws of Hell* and I will continue to give more teachings to complement it.

"*Namecha ikanzeyo.*" This Japanese phrase may be difficult to translate, so I would say, "Don't underestimate us!" Do not take religion lightly. At least in recorded human history, religion has existed at least for several thousands of years. This is because it contains something real. If it did not, religion, itself, would have perished long ago. It would have been long gone if people only considered cutting costs or holding back on donations so that they could make ends meet. The reason religion does not perish is that the other world really exists. This being so, we must ask the following questions, "If the other world exists, what should we do? How should we live?"

Whether you will go to heaven or hell depends on you being "heliocentric" or "geocentric"

What religion is saying is very simple. I will narrow it down to the most essential points. What I actually want to say is, faith is the most important. However, since some people in the audience still have a shallow understanding of religion, I will put this on hold. These people may take their time cultivating their faith, but here is what I would like to say to them beforehand. If you think that the world exists for you or if you have an excessive desire for self-preservation, then unfortunately, you will not be able to go to the world of heaven. This is also true for people who think that only they should succeed, prosper, and attain happiness or pleasure. On the other hand, if you wish to live for the happiness of others and live to make the world better, even by just a little, you will go to heaven. It is as simple as this.

There are two theoretical models to describe the structure of the solar system: geocentrism and heliocentrism. Geocentrism refers to the idea that the Sun and the planets revolve around the Earth. If you take this view and think that everyone revolves around you like how the Sun and other celestial bodies revolve around the Earth, and you stay put at the center as if you are the Earth, then you will go to hell. But if you take the heliocentric view and believe that "the Earth" is the one revolving around "the Sun," then you will go to heaven. This mindset is the condition for entering heaven.

This makes sense, though. As you live on Earth, do you feel that the Earth is making a full rotation every 24 hours? You would think that, if that is true, it would be so windy to live on the Earth that you would be blown away and thrown into outer space. Indeed for a long time, humans believed that the Sun revolved around the Earth, saying, "Just watch the Sun, and you will clearly see that it always rises from the east and sets in the west." But the reality was different, which was made clear once humans traveled to outer space. Similarly, the fact is clear in the eyes of those who can see this world from the perspective of the Spirit World. There is no room for doubt.

Here is what will happen to geocentric people and heliocentric people. Those who think that the world exists for them or revolves around them will likely go to hell, whereas those who think that they must take action for the world will likely go to heaven. Please remember this. Therefore, people who think that earthly pleasures are all and everything will, unfortunately, be met with harsh consequences after finding out that they still have life even after death.

"Hell on earth" is now being created

Materialism and scientism are prevalent in the world and are spreading in the field of education as well. I am not sure if there is anyone who has the right to do this, but if someone were to scientifically conclude that the other world and spirits do not exist—which seems to be the current general trend, though—then they would face serious consequences.

If you think that souls and the other world do not exist, and you are happy with this world because manufacturers are rapidly producing new goods one after another to make it convenient to live in, then you will have nowhere to go after you die because this earthly world is the only world you know of. What I mean is, I have long been saying that heaven and hell exist, but it seems that there are now more than these two worlds in the afterlife. This is what I am seeing. Many people who only believe that this third dimension is all there is are dying one after another. But they have nowhere to go after death, so they remain in this world and think that this "ground surface" is their home—I guess there are buildings, so it may be rude to say they are living on the ground. There are elevators, too, so it cannot exactly be called the ground, but in any case, the spirits of such people think that this world is their home, so they neither go to heaven nor hell. These spirits are increasing every year. This is a serious problem.

They are in the fourth dimension, but they can see the people living in this world. They can see the buildings. They can see you working and hear your voice. But their words cannot be heard by people like you who live in this third dimension. Only a small portion of people can see spirits; they can see and hear spirits, but other people cannot confirm it. Scientifically speaking, this is something that cannot be verified because science assumes that something is true only if the experiment shows the same result every time and for every person.

So, many spirits of those who died are still in this world. They are attached to their families, their workplace, or the place where they died. That is why "hell on earth," which is another world aside from heaven and hell, has now formed. The number of spirits going there is increasing greatly. What can we do about this?

Lost spirits are coexisting in this world with humans. They are "living" in this world. I am sure this causes a lot of trouble to all of you; you may be experiencing numerous problems. We need to reduce the number of these spirits. I want those spirits who can return to heaven to go to heaven, and for those who cannot to decide on which hell they should go to and properly undergo spiritual training there. Then, they must decide for themselves in hell, whether they will live as a devil forever or go back to heaven.

To use an example from a South Korean TV drama, I am asking you, will you go toward God or Park Il-do? You must choose one or the other. Park Il-do is a devil-like spirit that appears in a popular Korean TV drama. You do not have to watch it, but in this drama, Park Il-do is like a commander of devils, and he goes on a killing spree. I have watched a few episodes, so I could not help but mention it here. Such a devil does not actually exist, but in any case, it is a symbol or an icon. Such a character is portrayed in the drama. People in South Korea are at least aware that a devil-like being exists, which is good. A story that depicts a deceased person going on to become a lost spirit and making the people in this world unhappy is aired on TV. This alone is a great thing. In this way, South Korea has a better environment to understand spiritual matters than Japan. Maybe, it is because they are put in a position to be conscious of death.

This world is now overflowing with the spirits of people who do not realize that they are, indeed, dead and can go to neither heaven nor hell. Among them, many are those who had high educational background or were scientists and considered themselves "smart." Many of them were also rich. We want to reduce the number of such lost spirits. Otherwise, the law that governs this world and the next would not work as it should.

Strive to make the happiness in this world meet the happiness in the other world

In conclusion, what "Making the Way to True Salvation" means is to clearly establish the rule that applies both in this world and the other world. That is to say, happiness in this world must lead to happiness in the other world. To achieve this, I have written over 3,100 books. I have accumulated this much, yet these teachings are still far from reaching the whole world. I will keep working, but the world population is growing so fast that my teachings are still far from reaching all people. That is why it is all the more important for us to spread the teachings further, even if we can only make one or two steps forward at a time.

"Making the Way to True Salvation" or the purpose of religion is to make the happiness in this world meet the happiness in the other world. This is it.

CHAPTER THREE

Overcoming the Crisis of Earth
—A Lecture on *The Laws of Hell*

Originally recorded in Japanese on January 8, 2023
at Tokyo Shoshinkan of Happy Science in Tokyo, Japan
and later translated into English.

1

The Consequence of Thinking That Life Ends at Death

The reason I published *The Laws of Hell*

I hesitate to say "Happy New Year" because from what I can foresee, this year (2023) isn't looking too good. However, we should be thankful that we are able to see each other like this alive. We are in very tough times, indeed. I never imagined I would be lecturing on *The Laws of Hell* from the start of the year. But I am grateful for the simple fact that I am able to hold this event with you.

Last December, the Japanese Diet was discussing if people who made offerings to religion—because they were threatened that they would fall to hell if they refused—should be able to get their money back. In a time like this, Happy Science confidently published *The Laws of Hell*. This itself shows our strong determination. We have no concern over what the Diet says. This is how bold we are. What is more, in addition to publishing *The Laws of Hell* and a lecture on it that I am giving today, I also thought of writing a novel called *The Hell Monk* and spent the year-end and New Year's holidays working on it. The novel is even more radical than the content of *The Laws of Hell* and will be published soon. (*The Hell Monk* was published on January 19, 2023. Available only in Japanese.)

Let's say we asked people on the street, "Do you think hell exists?" or "Do you think you might go to hell after death?" I wonder how many will say, "Yes, I think so." Will there even be 20 percent? Probably not. If we were to take a poll, the majority would deny hell because their "common view" is worldly or materialistic. I cannot imagine that the number of people who believe in hell will exceed 50 percent in this day and age.

In reality, contrary to what people are thinking, the number of people falling to hell is rapidly increasing. For this reason, we, Happy Science, will continue to say what must be said regardless of what is discussed in the Diet, reported in the news, or written in newspapers. Even if 99 percent of people in the world think I am crazy, I will continue preaching about what I believe is right.

That is why, the audience at this main venue (Tokyo Shoshinkan) today was made up of our devotee members only. When there are all kinds of people in the audience, I find it difficult to say certain things. Just having people from the mass media makes things difficult.

Today, I may say things that will touch a sore spot, but please know that I mean well. Rather than learning about the pain after you fall off a cliff, wouldn't it be better to learn about it before you fall? I would not call this a threat. I am telling you this as a caution or a warning.

In the Preface of *The Laws of Hell*, I humbly wrote about myself, "Who can write such a book in this modern age? There is only one person." I believe it is OK for me to write one book like this after having written as many as 3,100. It would certainly be a little scary if this were my first book. But since I have written so many more, I think people will understand if I tell them to criticize me only after they have read other books of mine.

Before this lecture started, the song *The Prophet* (words and music by Ryuho Okawa) was played. The lyrics of the song were originally a poem that I wrote while I was a layman; in other words, I wrote it during my last years of "hiding" before I rose as a religious leader and founded Happy Science. I was in a period of struggle, trying to see if I could really make it on my own. Just as it is written in the poem, if all I had to do was be "breastfed by God," that would have been easier, but my work was much heavier than I imagined. I, myself, was not sure whether I would really be able to bear the responsibility and was going through a strong inner conflict.

On the contrary, younger people today are quite the opposite. Many of them want to attain a higher position fast and become "gods" quickly. But in reality, God's work is very heavy. It takes a lot of will and courage to be able to publish *The Laws of Hell* confidently and make it a bestseller when the lawmakers are discussing in the Diet, "If religions threaten or brainwash their believers by saying they will go to hell, they will have to return their offerings retrospectively, going back as far as over 10 years." No one can publish such a book without the determination to keep on fighting, even if it means making the whole world your enemy.

What I want to say is, what is right is right. There are certainly wrong religions in this world, and indeed, the religious group that is currently under discussion in the Diet is one of them. But please be assured that there are truths that you can believe that are being taught in the world of religions. So we must keep teaching the truth.

I have criticized the religion that is now in question as being misguided in some of my books. Nevertheless, what exists, exists. I believe now is the time for me to repeatedly tell people that, "What we say is not made up. What exists, truly exists."

Graveyards make people think about the afterlife

The reason is in particular, I get a strong sense of feeling that this world is becoming more like hell. The world we are living in is full of material goods and has become more convenient. So, it seems that people only care about living a fulfilling and happy life in this world and do not care about the afterlife. More and more people have such values. They probably think that hell should only appear in, for example, the world of anime. This is how much the other world has been downplayed, but I am saying that the reality is quite different.

In this world, material things have developed greatly and some of those things are actually necessary for us to live. That is why we have the role of making, growing, selling, and buying various things as we live in this world.

However, under such circumstances, we must not forget that the essence of human beings is the soul and that we are spiritual beings. There are fewer and fewer people who talk about this, and this is actually a problem.

On my way here today, I saw some graveyards and I thought to myself, "Oh, there are still graveyards in this area. They haven't been taken down. I wonder when condominiums will take over." More and more graveyards are being replaced. On my way to Tokyo Shoshinkan, I used to see a lot of graveyards, but most of them have now become condominiums and I believe it is because they make more profit.

However, graveyards and cemeteries remind people of the afterlife. They provide them with an opportunity to think, "Perhaps the other world really exists." There are also various religious events such as *Obon* (a Japanese Buddhist tradition that commemorates and remembers deceased ancestors), *meinichi* (memorial services on the anniversary of a person's death), and the New Year. People may think that these traditional events are nonsense or are mere customs. But still, they give people opportunities to think that the other world may really exist after death.

These customs and graveyards are slowly disappearing. Nowadays, to save money, more and more people wish to have their ashes scattered, for example, in Tokyo Bay from a cruiser or around a tree in a park. Indeed, they can save millions of yen that way because they do not need a tomb or a funeral. But when these people die and become spirits, they will have no idea as to what to do or where to go. I see a tremendous number of such lost spirits these days.

Such spirits grew up being told that everything ends with death as a common belief. This led them to lead a materialistic life. When they die, they will not be able to comprehend their own death because they do not believe in the afterlife. Spirits who believe that they are not dead will have no place to go. Since they have nowhere to return to, they will go to their office, home, or hospital that they used to be at when they were alive. That is why many spirits tend to wander around in those places.

Some of you may work in a hospital. In many cases, hospitals in hell are overlapping with hospitals in this third dimensional world. Many spirits of the patients who died there are wandering about, and so are the spirits of the doctors and nurses who used to work there when they were alive. I see many living and dead people being "hospitalized" together in the same space. We can expect this to happen in an abandoned hospital or a closed hospital as depicted in horror films, but this is also happening in hospitals that are currently in business. I hope hospitals with staff who know the Truth are not in the same terrible situation.

These spirits do not have a place to go. They did not learn about, hear about, or believe in the afterlife when they were alive. We cannot find anything about it in newspapers or TV news, and neither do school textbooks cover it. Sometimes the TV or newspapers report on the memorial service of the war dead on August 15th or the Hiroshima Peace Ceremony. But they probably thought that the news had nothing to do with them.

So, here is what I want to tell you. Many things have been developed to help us improve our physical condition and maintain our health, such as medicine, food, exercise methods, and healthcare goods. These things have made this world easier for us to live in, which is fine. But what you must do is not allow these things to make you forget the important things. That is, we must not forget our spirituality and spiritual matters.

2

Heaven and Hell Exist Even Now

Spirits in the Hell of Hungry Ghosts are full of insatiable hunger

The Hell of Hungry Ghosts has existed since ancient times. In present-day Japan, it is rare for people to starve to death, so their number is quite small. For example, an elderly man, who lived alone, had no one to look after him during his last days and was found a few days after his death, may have died of hunger. Apart from cases like this, not many people starve to death, including homeless people. So, it may be difficult to imagine what the Hell of Hungry Ghosts is like.

In the past, however, many people were unable to eat because of various reasons including famine. That is why they became hungry ghosts. They are thin but have protruding bellies, just like the people we still see in the poorer areas around the world.

As written in the Buddhist scriptures, the moment these hungry ghosts try to put food in their mouth, it burns away instantly, so they are unable to eat. This phenomenon symbolizes their dissatisfaction. Even if they put food in their mouth and think that they ate it, they can never feel satisfied. They constantly feel dissatisfied however many times they eat. This is the reality of people who died of starvation.

How to avoid being possessed by the spirits of hell

Recently, especially after we started communicating with Red Punisher, or ogre (of Kusatsu), we have been taught a lot about the harsh reality concerning the relationship between men and women. The average age of all of you here today is a little over 50, so this topic may no longer bother you, and you may say, "Master, we don't mind whether you are strict or tolerant. Please tell us the truth." On the other hand, people in their 20s may say, "My life will be affected greatly depending on what you say, Master, so please do not take it as a trifling issue." At any rate, if people are too obsessed with having sexual intercourse with the opposite sex, thinking that it is the most valuable thing, then their view of life will become less and less spiritual. This is the biggest problem.

People who have a strong craving for the opposite sex during their life on earth will become lustful ghosts after they die and return to the other world. The lustful feelings they had when they were alive, or their sexual desires, will linger in them even after they die. And even if they seek out the opposite sex in the other world, they cannot be satisfied because they no longer have a physical body. Just as hungry ghosts cannot eat anything, lustful ghosts cannot feel sexual pleasure no matter how much they try.

What do they do then? Some of them sneak out of hell and possess people who are enjoying themselves in the red-light districts of this world or possess the youth who are crazy for the opposite sex. They can possess these people based on the Law of the Same Wavelengths. When people are possessed by lustful ghosts, their sexual desires become even stronger.

When spirits possess the people of this world, they experience a sensation that is somewhat similar to what they used to experience when they were living as humans. It is not a real sensation, but they can vaguely experience the feeling. That is why they sneak out of hell to possess the people of this world. However, if people on earth are able to control their minds, that is to reflect on their thoughts as soon as their sexual desire arises and quickly regain peace of mind, then they will no longer be possessed by lustful spirits because their wavelengths will not attune to those spirits. This is the Law of the Same Wavelengths.

So, here is what I want to tell people in their 20s and 30s. Please examine carefully whether it is you, yourself, who is seeking the opposite sex, or whether you are provoked to do so because you are possessed and that is why you crave it. If you have lost control of yourself and you have become a "tool" for other beings to use, then that is shameful as a human being. It means you are not the one in control of your actions. So, please check this point by asking yourself, "Am I the one thinking this, or is it someone else?"

Differences in the descriptions of hell between religions

I just gave you a few examples of the worlds of hell. Without a doubt, heaven and hell do exist. This is a hard fact. The religion that teaches about hell in most detail is, indeed, Buddhism. Its descriptions of hell are the most detailed among the world religions.

Christianity, on the other hand, teaches very little about hell. Christians are aware of evil spirits, malicious spirits, or devils that come to possess the people in this world because they have exorcists to cast out such beings. But exorcists are dealing with evil spirits that have come to this world from hell to make people go insane. They practice exorcism to drive out evil spirits that try to kill people or make people commit suicide, but in terms of what the world of hell is actually like, Christians do not know much. Christianity does not have enough teachings on hell. Jesus only had as little as three years or so to preach the teachings so he could not teach enough about hell to people.

When Jesus taught about hell, he said something like, "Those who fall to hell will be burnt by the eternal *gouka* or the flames of karma." Because he described it like that, many Christians believe that they will never be able to come out of hell once they have fallen there. They think of hell as such a place. This implies that the souls in hell will practically perish. So, the only way for people to enter the gate of life is by having Christian belief and becoming a Christian. In a nutshell, this is what Christianity teaches.

On top of that, to help their missionary activity, they later added the idea that "people can *only* be saved by Christianity." This was probably done by Jesus' disciples. But since this idea implies that the believers of other religions cannot be saved and have no place to go after death, Christians came up with the idea of purgatory. According to Christianity, purgatory is the world that exists between heaven and hell, where heretics who died and left this world are "pooled" for a certain period of time. Those who repent, seek help in Christianity and have devoted themselves to its teachings will ascend to heaven and be saved. Christians invented this intermediate world. In *The Divine Comedy*, Dante also writes about Heaven, Purgatory, and Hell.

On the other hand, there is no concept of purgatory in Buddhism. From the Christian perspective, the description of the worlds of hell in Buddhism all sound like purgatory. Buddhism teaches that even if people fall to hell after death, they will be able to ascend to heaven if they reflect enough on their thoughts and deeds and repent of their mistakes. So, hell in the Buddhist context is, in a way, similar to purgatory in Christianity.

Hell in the Christian context would be the depths of hell in Buddhist terms. Spirits who have been in the depths of hell for 1,000 to 2,000 years as devils cannot easily ascend to heaven, so it might be true to say that such spirits will never be able to ascend. They have done such great evil to humankind that they may never be able to ascend to heaven. But in principle, Buddhism teaches that humans can be saved through faith. Faith and self-reflection are vital. People can be saved by having faith and reflecting on their past thoughts and deeds. This is the difference between Buddhism and Christianity. So you could say that Christianity is somewhat premature compared to Buddhism.

Islam does not give enough descriptions of the Spirit World either, probably because Muhammad did not have many spiritual experiences. In Islam, hell is not described clearly; only an evil spirit called "Jinn" appears in their teachings. They also teach that if you believe in Islam and make efforts to live your life righteously, you can return to heaven, where a river of wine is flowing. Hmm, "a river of wine," huh? They also say that beautiful virgins are waiting for you near the river. Hmm, is that really heaven? It sounds a little suspicious to me. Considering that Islam is a religion that was founded in the desert, maybe it is a good thing for them to have a river of wine flowing, but having "beautiful virgins waiting" makes me doubt if they are mistaking heaven for a hostess bar. This description of heaven is a little suspicious. Since Muhammad also studied Christian teachings, perhaps Muslims were somewhat influenced by Christian ideas as well. In any case, seeing their descriptions of heaven and hell, I feel that the teachings of Islam are not up to par, either.

The religion that clearly describes hell in most detail is Buddhism. It is also the only religion that clearly teaches what will cause people to go to hell, and how they can ascend to heaven from there, according to the law of cause and effect. But because these teachings are taught in old languages such as classical Chinese, they must be taught again in modern languages. That is what I am doing.

3

The Reason for Torment in Hell

Different kinds of hell exist to teach souls that they are spiritual entities

In reality, there are many different kinds of hell. Some of them reflect the modern age, but anyhow, all sorts of hell exist even now. For example, there is a hell where the souls are boiled in a cauldron as punishment. Historically in Japan, criminals were sometimes executed by being thrown into a cauldron that contained boiling water, as also depicted in folk tales. Originally in China, they used boiling oil, but since oil was precious and rare in Japan, hot water was commonly used. When water is heated up, it only goes up to 100 degrees Celsius. People will certainly die if they are thrown in boiling water. But if thrown in oil, they will be deep fried as the oil heats up to hundreds of degrees. People who are thrown into the boiling oil will be fried crispy, so this would be a much harsher punishment than being thrown into boiling water. Folk tales sometimes depict a cauldron like that.

Being boiled in a cauldron as punishment is harsh, indeed, but in the end, this is a lesson that is necessary for the souls who believe that they are nothing more than physical existences. If they realize that they are not physical bodies but spiritual beings, they will not feel the heat. Because they believe that they are just their physical bodies, they are just thinking that being boiled would be horrible and terribly hot. This is the point.

The same is true with the Mountain of Needles. In this hell, souls are forced to climb a mountain of needles or walk through a field of swords and knives as they are chased by ogres (punishers). There is also the Hell of the Bloody Pond, where souls are swimming, floating, or drowning in the bloody pond. All of these hells exist to teach souls, who think based on their belief that they are physical bodies, to change their way of thinking. It is to guide them to realize that they can never die in the truest sense. This is the first level of enlightenment for the souls in hell, and for them to awaken to this truth, such phenomena occur in hell.

Some worlds of hell have become more modernized. One example is the Hell of Black Cords. The black cords are inked cords. Carpenters used them in the old times to draw a straight line on wood. They would then saw along it. According to ancient Buddhist scriptures, the souls who have fallen in the Hell of Black Cords have their bodies marked with inked cords and sawed by ogres along the lines.

Let's say that you are sentenced to 500 years in the Hell of Black Cords to be sawed. When you think about it, it is tough for souls to have their bodies sawed for 500 years in the Hell of Black Cords, but it is also tough for the ogres who have to saw for 500 years. It would be very strenuous work; even professional wrestlers would not be able to do this. For this reason, some hells are modernized and they look and function like how a hospital does. In those hells, things like electric saws are used, although machinery does not actually exist in the Spirit World. Hospitals nowadays use electric saws to cut open the skull, so the same kind of device now appears in hell to the souls who have this knowledge.

But basically, what is happening in hell is all the same. In reality, the things I explained above are not real and do not exist. It is the fear that the souls have that makes them appear as if they are real. Nowadays, there is even something like the Mountain of Syringe Needles.

That is why it is very important to have a spiritual view of life, which Happy Science teaches. It will help you realize your mistakes faster. You will also be able to realize where you went wrong much sooner, so please study it.

The true meaning of making offerings

I also teach the Laws of Success. There are many ways to make money, but unfortunately, you cannot bring money with you to the other world. You cannot take it with you and you cannot bribe Yama, the Special Judge of Hell, to let you off the hook. Sadly, no matter how much money you have accumulated in this world, you cannot bring it with you and give it to Yama, saying, "Please pardon my wrongdoings." Making money is exciting and it gives you a sense of success, but you must do it knowing that you cannot bring money back with you to the other world when you die. There is nothing wrong with making money as long as you are doing it so you can continue doing good work. Also, it is good to do it with gratitude, thinking, "It is a blessing that I can make a profit and pay salaries to support my employees and many other people" while you live in this world. You just need to keep in mind that, in the end, you cannot take money back with you to the other world.

The topic of offerings was a social issue last year (in Japan). When I saw people discussing this issue in the same manner as discussing a mere consumer contract, I realized that those people really did not understand the meaning of making offerings. Everyone likes to receive things from others. Whether it is food or money, they are happy when they are given it. On the other hand, people are not so happy when they have to give something away. That is why it is said that making offerings or practicing Happiness Planting is a form of spiritual discipline. Giving away what you have, whether it is one-tenth or however much, may make you feel as if you are losing out, so you probably do not feel like doing so. This is why making offerings is a part of spiritual discipline. It is different from consumption which is an activity under the supervision of the Consumer Affairs Agency.

Suppose you went to a shrine on New Year's Day and prayed so that you could pass the university entrance exam. You offered ¥10,000 in the offering box, which is a far greater amount compared to the money you usually offer because you really wanted to pass the exam. But when March came or the day of the exam result came, you found out that you failed all of them and did not pass a single university. When something like this happens, you may become outraged and even go to the shrine to protest, "Give me back my money! I prayed and made a lot of offerings, but I wasn't accepted by any university. You're a scam. I demand a refund!" However, your complaint will not be accepted because the exam result will be determined according to the efforts you made, and your level of ability from an objective standpoint. The efforts made by other students who took the exam will also be considered.

While it is not a bad thing to pray for success, what is essential is that you are making efforts toward what you have pledged to God. And when you receive the result, you must humbly accept it. If you have failed because of a lack of effort, you must reflect on that. Then, you can decide whether you will try again or move onto another path that allows you to exert your abilities. The result shows God's Will, telling you, "You must decide on your course."

Therefore, if people think that in a constitutional state, the laws are almighty and are like God, then I want to tell them that they are wrong. The word "Laws" in *The Laws of Hell* is different from the laws created in the Diet. The Laws that I preach are "Laws that cannot be changed," whereas laws made by humans are laws created through the majority vote. Please bear this in mind.

4

How to Prevent a World War

The reality of the coronavirus infection in China

As it is the start of the new year, I must also talk about the direction that humanity should head toward or the ways of thinking we should have from now on.

It has been three years since the coronavirus pandemic broke out. About three years ago, when the number of infected cases was still around 10,000 or so worldwide, I predicted that the number would reach an astronomical figure. And this has become a reality.

Now, it is almost impossible to find out the real number of infected cases in each country because they are all hiding it and not telling the truth. Before China's statistics came out, it was said that more than 600 million people were infected around the world. Then, in mid-December of last year, the documents that were leaked from the Chinese authorities revealed that 250 million people were infected in China. However, those are only the reported number of cases, meaning, no less than 250 million people are infected; the actual number could be twice or more than that. In fact, over 60 percent of the people in Sichuan Province are said to be infected. When two planes from China flew into Italy and the passengers were tested for COVID, it was reported that more than 50 percent of the Chinese tourists were already infected. From this, we can assume that over half of the Chinese population has been infected by coronavirus. Since there are 1.4 billion people in China, it would mean that about 700 to 800 million people have been infected. I do not know the actual number of infected cases in the world, but it may have reached between one and two billion (at the time of the lecture). Even so, this is still within my expectations. I predict that, at the most, the number of infected cases could reach four billion, or half the world's population. So, the number could still go up.

Japan is now seeing its eighth wave of the pandemic. It was initially reported that the current coronavirus variant was highly contagious, like the flu, but that its fatality rate was low. But then, near the end of last year, experts started saying that the fatality rate is 15 to 16 times more than that of the previous year (2021). I am not sure if it is realistic for it to be 15 to 16 times higher. It could be that various coronavirus-related deaths were only recently included in the statistics. I do not know how the numbers are altered on this matter, but the fatality rate is indeed rising.

The future forecast of the pandemic

From the outset, I suspected that this pandemic was a virus war, so I have been saying since the beginning that the coronavirus was spread by a specific country. It is clear that the coronavirus was created using a virus taken from bats that inhabit the caves located about 2,000 km (about 1,200 miles) south of the Wuhan Institute of Virology. The DNA of the coronavirus is a mixture of the DNA of the bat-borne virus and the DNA of the virus that causes AIDS, which severely damages people's immune systems so that they have higher chances of dying. Therefore, the coronavirus is clearly man-made. Such a virus cannot be of natural origin. It was created as a weapon in a virology lab.

This is a weapon that people use before nuclear weapons. When a country knows that it cannot win in a nuclear war, it goes for a virus war that it can start without being caught. This is how it goes. I knew from the beginning that this was the case with the pandemic. The culprit probably intended to start the pandemic secretively, but at the end of 2019, there was a sudden outbreak of the coronavirus that infected people at a fish market in Wuhan. Around the same time, at the end of December 2019, I obtained information from space people that the virus, which China had intended to scatter overseas, had "accidentally" leaked within the country. This was a warning given by the space people.

After that, China conducted a zero-COVID policy for a few years, but about a year ago, I conducted a "Coronavirus U-turn" prayer, like the "Yes, U-turn" prayer in my novel, *The Unknown Stigma 2* (New York: IRH Press, 2022). This was partially "leaked" in one of the spiritual messages I recorded last year. I actually conducted the prayer in secret to order the virus to go back to where it came from. If our members gathered and prayed together, we would be found out, so I did it secretly on my own. Then, the virus returned to China. However, if 700 to 800 million are infected, the virus may mutate and create new variants as it spreads among people of different Chinese ethnic groups. And, when many Chinese people travel around the world, in the case of Japan, we would be hit by the ninth wave. This is indeed possible, so I think the battle will continue.

I have said from the start that the pandemic would last about five years, so I believe there are two more years until it is over. But most probably, the Japanese media will intentionally report a lot of good news this year because they want things to get better. They will say things such as "an increased number of tourists," "restoration of businesses and an improved economy," and "year-end stock prices estimated to reach ¥30,000 or 40,000 (about US$200-270)." But please try not to be fooled by them so easily. More waves will come; the pandemic is not over yet. Please make sure to run a tight ship at your company or when doing your work. Things are still risky. You must continue to be on guard.

The conflict between rising groups

While the coronavirus war already has the characteristics of World War III, President Biden has made another bad move. Despite the fact that the virus came from China, ever since Mr. Biden became the president, the U.S. has virtually been in a state of war with Russia. In other words, they are fighting the wrong enemy. The U.S. lost 1.1 million of its people due to the coronavirus (at the time of the lecture). Surely a war would start when a country loses 1.1 million of its citizens. So it seems to me that the U.S. is waging a war against the wrong opponent.

Mr. Biden has made Russia his potential enemy instead and is fighting Russia via Ukraine because he "received a lot of bribes" from China. He has now formed the matchup, "NATO vs. Russia" and let China off the hook. So, this is a very complicated battle. I wonder if Mr. Biden is simply not very bright or if he really is evil. He could potentially be smart since he is the president of the U.S. I sometimes wonder if he only appears like an idiot because there is no one who is as smart as him to understand his intellect. He launched an attack on Russia when 1.1 million Americans died due to China's "coronavirus weapon." I wonder how his brain works.

The newspaper this morning (January 8, 2023) said that the U.S. would provide ¥400 billion (about US$2.6 billion) and send 50 tanks to assist Ukraine. So it made me think that he really wants to fight. When the strong attack the weak, people in general think that the strong are the ones to blame and that helping the weak is justice. This is the typical way people think. But if Ukraine continues to be given aid, without a doubt, this war that began last February will still continue until the end of the year. And if the war continues, more and more people will die. There will be many deaths since this is a war, meaning hell will form in both Russia and Ukraine. I believe many Hell of Agonizing Cries will be formed, which is not a good thing. I want them to agree to a cease-fire at some point, but it may not be so easy since the two countries have conflicting values.

Many people regard Mr. Zelensky as a hero, but I can hardly see him that way. I cannot help but feel that he is up to something very bad. As the president of Ukraine, it may be natural for him to ask other countries for help, but in my eyes, he seems very eager to start a world war. He gathers money and military supplies from other countries in the world to fight a proxy war against Russia. He asks other countries to support Ukraine by sending artillery, missiles, and tanks. This has urged Russia to make ties with countries like China, North Korea, and Iran. As a result, there are now two sets of countries that are in conflict. The structure of the Cold War is once again beginning to form, and this time, it is taking the shape of a world war. This is the worst-case scenario. The very worst is happening now, and it makes me sad to think that with the intellect of Mr. Biden, this is what happens. Japan is not the only country whose top leader lacks competence.

The Ukrainian president spoke with Japanese Prime Minister Kishida over the phone and asked him to come and see Ukraine. It is obvious that Mr. Kishida will "scatter money" as usual if he goes there, but if he does that, the war will never end. I believe it is better to put an end to the war as soon as possible.

Will nuclear weapons really be used?

Russia and Ukraine together used to be one single nation, so the war that is currently happening is not a battle between two foreign countries, as many are thinking. It is like two close relatives hating each other. There are many ethnic Russians in Ukraine. In the case of the former president of the Soviet Union, Mr. Gorbachev, his wife was Ukrainian. So, Ukraine is not really a foreign country to Russia, and vice versa.

I can understand Mr. Zelensky's personal desire to join the EU, but to expand NATO means to contain Russia. It would work as an advantage for the U.S. because it can create a strategy to destroy Russia using NATO. So it was obvious that Russia would be against it. Despite that, Mr. Zelensky prioritized his personal feelings. I think he was unable to see the big picture. Most certainly, the war would not have started if Ukraine had declared its neutrality.

What would happen now if someone were to recommend a cease-fire? When Mr. Hashimoto, a former politician who used to serve as the governor and the mayor of Osaka, said that it would be better for this war to come to a cease-fire, his comment apparently blew up on the Internet. My opinion, on the other hand, does not "blow up," even if I suggest a cease-fire since I do not use the Internet and my information comes from a totally different source.

How far will this war go? Should the U.S. send its army in this proxy war, I am sure that Russia will ultimately use nuclear weapons. As I have been saying since last year, there is an extremely high possibility that Russia will use them sometime this year. They will probably use tactical nuclear weapons first.

In fact, during the Russian Orthodox Christmas, Russia was calling for a cease-fire. Ukraine is also a Russian Orthodox country, which means that people who believe in the same religion are fighting each other. I believe this move was a sign, so I think it is time for them to figure out ways to come to an agreement. If humanity chooses to polarize the world and confront each other, it means that the current civilization has entered its period of destruction. In that case, things may get as worse as they can get.

My prediction is that if Ukraine continues to ask for and receive aid, it will eventually perish. The country, itself, will surely perish. What comes next would be a crisis for the EU. Countries of the EU will have to desperately defend themselves to make sure they will not collapse. Regarding Mr. Biden, his basic stance is to just give a little assistance from a safe place. In other words, he doesn't care if other countries lose because it doesn't bring any harm to the U.S. This is a very dangerous situation.

5

The World Situation up to 2050 and the Mission of Happy Science

The worst-case scenario that Japan should avoid

People often see the situation regarding this issue (the proxy war that is taking place between Russia and Ukraine) as the same problem as what Taiwan, South Korea, and Japan are now facing. Many Japanese right-wing journalists and commentators also think along the same lines and say, "We are disappointed in Happy Science and the Happiness Realization Party. They are saying they would protect Taiwan from China, so they must also fight against Russia, but they are not. This is outrageous." So, it seems we are now opposed by both the right wing and the left wing.

But in simple words, what we are saying regarding this is that, if we analyze the military strength of the countries involved, the worst-case scenario for Japan today would be to fight against all three countries, North Korea, China, and Russia. Such a situation must be avoided at all costs.

Japan has Article 9 of the Constitution (renunciation of war) and does not possess any nuclear weapons, but these three countries do. So, Japan must never make an enemy of all three countries at the same time.

Japan should have kept with Mr. Abe's diplomatic policy and brought Russia on Japan's side by all means. If Japan can do so, China will not be able to make a move against Japan so easily because Russia, a country with nuclear weapons, will be supporting Japan. China will not be able to dominate the world. That is why I have been saying that we must not let Russia and China join hands. But the Japanese government officials are incompetent and do not understand what I mean. I guess it can't be helped. After all, Japan may be heading toward the worst-case scenario.

Future forecast for North Korea and China

Having said that, let me tell you what I sense from the current situation.

Indeed, the country of Ukraine will most probably be wiped out, if the West chooses to continue supplying weapons to Ukraine and refuses to agree to a cease-fire, making Zelensky a hero. But if I may add one thing, I believe that North Korea will also disappear. The U.S. will not allow North Korea to do as they like. A small country of about 20 million people that now possesses both atomic and hydrogen bombs is frequently shooting missiles and is going to shoot nuclear missiles next. Its missiles can even target the U.S. military bases and the U.S. mainland. Considering such facts, North Korea will surely be destroyed, though I cannot say when. If Kim Jong-un gives up on what he is doing now and opens up North Korea to the world, they still have a way to be saved. But if he continues his deed to make North Korea more powerful, the country will likely perish.

So, my prediction is that, unless Ukraine changes its current course of action, it will perish. In addition, the country of North Korea will certainly be destroyed as well. Both countries will disappear from the face of the Earth.

As for China, on the other hand, the country itself will not perish. But now that the coronavirus has started spreading there, it is clear that China's hardline policy to contain the virus has failed. The possible resignation of Xi Jinping is also rumored. It seems that the Chinese people are beginning to have doubts, perhaps because the coronavirus started spreading again and because when they watched the World Cup, they saw that the people in the audience were not wearing masks. I believe there will soon be a rise of people in China who seek freedom, democracy, and faith, which the Happiness Realization Party advocates. Also, the country will be split into several parts: for example, the South and North of China, Xinjiang Uyghur Autonomous Region, Tibet Autonomous Region, Inner Mongolia Autonomous Region, and so on. Although the country itself will not be destroyed, chaos will follow for a while, and it will no longer be a monolithic country like how it is now.

We will ultimately win by around 2050

In drawing up the blueprint for the future, we must consider the possibility of the world population declining from eight billion to about four billion by 2050. We are currently in the year 2023, so that is about 27 years from now. While taking this into account, we are trying to change the direction that the world is heading in.

In my early lectures, I said that the world population was five billion, so it has increased by three billion since then. In Kounosuke Matsushita's book that I was reading, he said that there were three billion people in the world. Back then, the world population was still three billion, so that means it has now increased by five billion. If these five billion people think that this earthly world is the only world there is and seek worldly territory, worldly convenience, and materialistic prosperity only, then some kind of power will come into play. This power will not allow Earthlings to do whatever they want.

It is God's plan for humans to undergo soul training by repeatedly being reborn on earth. Viewed from the cosmic perspective, the planet Earth is an extremely precious place for educating souls. So we will put an end to the current problems by around 2050 and ultimately win.

Nevertheless, it will take a little more time for that to happen. My wife has been urging me to work until I am at least 90 years old, and if possible, until 95. If I work until I am 93 or so, the year 2050 will come. She even asks me to live until I am 100, even when all I can do is exist and do nothing else. I may be giving lectures from my wheelchair in my 90s, but it does not make much difference whether

I speak standing up or sitting down. As long as my mind is clear, I can give lectures. I feel I should hang in there as much as I can, so I will do my best.

In addition, I have decided to extend the retirement age of Happy Science staff, although our believers may become upset because it will be a heavier burden on them. Some of them might complain, "We should just send incompetent monks back to secular life as soon as possible." Generally, in society, many employees retire at age 60. Even if they were to extend their retirement age, it would usually be up to 65. But I do not think it is a good thing to have many monks and nuns resign, only to live on a public pension. Happy Science must be independent. We cannot express what we want to say unless we can support ourselves to a certain extent, so we want to be an independent organization as much as possible.

For religious professionals, it is often the case that, their value goes up as they get older. The audience here today is not that old, but still, the average age is over 50. If the branch managers are all in their 20s or 30s, our older members may hesitate to, for example, ask for life counseling or to listen to their sermons. But we also have many staff who have now been working for 30 years or more. They may no longer be good at using electronics or doing paperwork, but since they are older and more experienced than younger staff, they are better at giving lectures or life counseling. Also, the ritual prayers they conduct and the sutras they recite are more effective. So, I would like these people to remain as Happy Science staff for as long as possible.

For this reason, the retirement age for our staff is very different or on a completely different level from the usual age in society. Our staff will retire at 75. Those in management positions will retire at 80, and they can extend this to 85 if they are still capable and healthy. I am making these arrangements because I plan to work until 90. If there are only staff who are 60 years old and younger when I am 90, I will be quite lonely and it will be hard to bear. I need some of the older staff to stay, and they would be indeed helpful. People will listen humbly to the lecturing or scolding of someone who is 60, 70, or 80 years old. In this way, age plays an important factor. Although our staff are paid little, I decided to have them work for as long as possible and not live on tax money. This is our policy. In this way, we are determined to win the battle by 2050. So I would like you to support us.

We will continue to fight to right the wrong in the world

This year (2023), we will carry out activities that are mainly based on *The Laws of Hell*. It is time we change our society. Not even 20 percent of the general public believe that hell exists. They are wrong to believe so. It is a solemn fact that hell exists, so we must correct this mistaken belief.

You cannot learn about hell in school textbooks, and if you ask the schoolteachers, they will probably deny its existence. Japan's Ministry of Education, Culture, Sports, Science and Technology knows nothing about it, either. It said things like, "Your school was established by a religion that publishes spiritual messages, so it is not academic." This is a misjudgment that is so sinful that calls for a death sentence. However, this modern age does not allow for this to happen.

The world must not continue as it is, so I will keep on firing "bullets of Truth" for another 30 to 40 years. We, Happy Science, have local branches and temples overseas, but they are still weak. We need to make them much, much stronger. Should new religions, or even traditional religions such as Christianity, Buddhism, and Islam perish, Happy Science will keep fighting on and on. To that end, I ask for your strong support.

For a deeper understanding of
Faithful to the Truth
see other books below by Ryuho Okawa:

The Laws of Hell [New York: IRH Press, 2023]

The Unknown Stigma 2 [New York: IRH Press, 2022]

ABOUT THE AUTHOR

Founder and CEO of Happy Science Group.

Ryuho Okawa was born on July 7th 1956, in Tokushima, Japan. After graduating from the University of Tokyo with a law degree, he joined a Tokyo-based trading house. While working at its New York headquarters, he studied international finance at the Graduate Center of the City University of New York. In 1981, he attained Great Enlightenment and became aware that he is El Cantare with a mission to bring salvation to all humankind.

In 1986, he established Happy Science. It now has members in 170 countries across the world, with more than 700 branches and temples as well as 10,000 missionary houses around the world.

He has given over 3,500 lectures (of which more than 150 are in English) and published over 3,150 books (of which more than 600 are Spiritual Interview Series), many of which are translated into 42 languages. Along with *The Laws of the Sun* and *The Laws of Hell*, many of the books have become best sellers or million sellers. To date, Happy Science has produced 27 movies under his supervision. He has given the original story and concept and is also the Executive Producer. He has also composed music and written lyrics for over 450 pieces.

Moreover, he is the Founder of Happy Science University and Happy Science Academy (Junior and Senior High School), Founder and President of the Happiness Realization Party, Founder and Honorary Headmaster of Happy Science Institute of Government and Management, Founder of IRH Press Co., Ltd., and the Chairperson of NEW STAR PRODUCTION Co., Ltd. and ARI Production Co., Ltd.

WHO IS EL CANTARE?

El Cantare means "the Light of the Earth." He is the Supreme God of the Earth who has been guiding humankind since the beginning of Genesis, and He is the Creator of the universe. He is whom Jesus called Father and Muhammad called Allah, and is *Ame-no-Mioya-Gami*, Japanese Father God. Different parts of El Cantare's core consciousness have descended to Earth in the past, once as Alpha and another as Elohim. His branch spirits, such as Shakyamuni Buddha and Hermes, have descended to Earth many times and helped to flourish many civilizations. To unite various religions and to integrate various fields of study in order to build a new civilization on Earth, a part of the core consciousness has descended to Earth as Master Ryuho Okawa.

Alpha is a part of the core consciousness of El Cantare who descended to Earth around 330 million years ago. Alpha preached Earth's Truths to harmonize and unify Earth-born humans and space people who came from other planets.

Elohim is a part of the core consciousness of El Cantare who descended to Earth around 150 million years ago. He gave wisdom, mainly on the differences between light and darkness, good and evil.

Ame-no-Mioya-Gami (Japanese Father God) is the Creator God and the Father God who appears in ancient literature, *Hotsuma Tsutae*. It is believed that He descended on the foothills of Mt. Fuji about 30,000 years ago and built the Fuji dynasty, which is the root of the Japanese civilization. With justice as the central pillar, Ame-no-Mioya-Gami's teachings spread to ancient civilizations of other countries in the world.

Shakyamuni Buddha was born as a prince into the Shakya clan in India around 2,600 years ago. When he was 29 years old, he renounced the world and sought enlightenment. He later attained Great Enlightenment and founded Buddhism.

Hermes is one of the 12 Olympian gods in Greek mythology, but the spiritual Truth is that he taught the teachings of love and progress around 4,300 years ago which became the origin of the current Western civilization. He is a hero who truly existed.

Ophealis was born in Greece around 6,500 years ago and was the leader who took an expedition to as far as Egypt. He is the God of miracles, prosperity, and arts, and is known as Osiris in Egyptian mythology.

Rient Arl Croud was born as a king of the ancient Incan Empire around 7,000 years ago and taught about the mysteries of the mind. In the heavenly world, he is responsible for the interactions that take place between various planets.

Thoth was an almighty leader who built the golden age of the Atlantic civilization around 12,000 years ago. In Egyptian mythology, he is known as God Thoth.

Ra Mu was a leader who built the golden age of the civilization of Mu around 17,000 years ago. As a religious leader and a politician, he ruled by uniting religion and politics.

ABOUT HAPPY SCIENCE

Happy Science is a religious group founded on the faith in El Cantare who is the God of the Earth, and the Creator of the universe. The essence of human beings is the soul that was created by God, and we all are children of God. God is our true parent, so in our souls, we have a fundamental desire to "believe in God, love God, and get closer to God." And, we can get closer to God by living with God's Will as our own. In Happy Science, we call this the "Exploration of Right Mind." More specifically, it means to practice the Fourfold Path, which consists of "Love, Wisdom, Self-Reflection, and Progress."

Love: Love means "love that gives," or mercy. God hopes for the happiness of all people. Therefore, living with God's Will as our own means to start by practicing "love that gives."

Wisdom: God's love is boundless. It is important to learn various Truths in order to understand the heart of God.

Self-Reflection: Once you learn the heart of God and the difference between His mind and yours, you should strive to bring your own mind closer to the mind of God— that process is called self-reflection. Self-reflection also includes meditation and prayer.

Progress: Since God hopes for the happiness of all people, you should also make progress in your love, and make an effort to realize utopia in which everyone in your society, country, and eventually all humankind can become happy.

As we practice this Fourfold Path, our souls will advance toward God step by step. That is when we can attain real happiness—our souls' desire to get closer to God comes true.

In Happy Science, we conduct activities to make ourselves happy through belief in Lord El Cantare, and to spread this faith to the world and bring happiness to all. We welcome you to join our activities!

We hold events and activities to help you practice the Fourfold Path at our branches, temples, missionary centers and missionary houses

Love: We hold various volunteering activities. Our members conduct missionary work together as the greatest practice of love.

Wisdom: We offer our comprehensive collection of books of Truth, many of which bookstores do not have available. In addition, we offer numerous opportunities such as seminars or book clubs to learn the Truth.

Self-Reflection: We offer opportunities to polish your mind through self-reflection, meditation, and prayer. Many members have experienced improvement in their human relationships by changing their own minds.

Progress: We also offer seminars to enhance your power of influence. Because it is also important to do well at work to make society better, we hold seminars to improve your work and management skills.

BOOKS BY RYUHO OKAWA

Laws Series

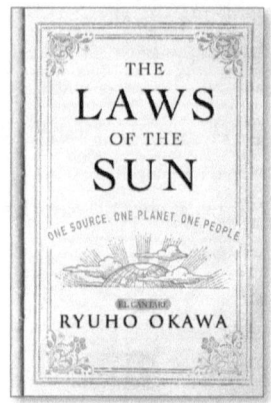

The Laws of the Sun

One Source, One Planet, One People

Paperback • 288 pages • $15.95
ISBN: 978-1-942125-43-3 (Oct. 25, 2018)

IMAGINE IF YOU COULD ASK GOD why He created this world and what spiritual laws He used to shape us, and everything around us. The truth behind the creation of the universe is revealed in this book. If we could understand His designs and intentions, we could discover what our goals in life should be and whether our actions move us closer to those goals or farther away.

At a young age, a spiritual calling prompted Ryuho Okawa to outline what he innately understood to be universal truths for all humankind. Ryuho Okawa outlines these laws of the universe and provides a road map for living one's life with greater purpose and meaning.

In this powerful book, Ryuho Okawa reveals the transcendent nature of consciousness and the secrets of our multidimensional universe and our place in it. By understanding the different stages of love and following the Buddhist Eightfold Path, he believes we can speed up our eternal process of development. *The Laws of the Sun* shows the way to realize true happiness—a happiness that continues from this world through the other.

The Laws of Eternity

El Cantare Unveils the Structure of the Spirit World

Paperback • 224 pages • $17.95
ISBN: 978-1-958655-16-0 (May 15, 2024)

"Where do we come from and where do we go after death?"

This unparalleled book offers us complete answers to life's most important questions that we all are confronted with at some point or another.

In *The Laws of Eternity*, author Ryuho Okawa takes us on a journey to the other world, a place where we came from and return to after death. The other world has a multidimensional structure consisting of the worlds of the fourth, fifth, sixth, seventh, eighth, and ninth dimensions, where souls with the same level of spiritual awareness and similar characteristics reside.

This book reveals the eternal mysteries and the ultimate secrets of Earth's Spirit Group that have been covered by the veil of legends and myths. Encountering the long-hidden Eternal Truths that are revealed for the first time in human history will change the way you live your life now.

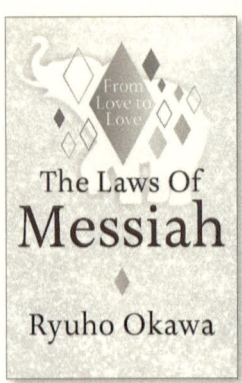

The Laws Of Messiah

From Love to Love

Paperback • 248 pages • $16.95
ISBN: 978-1-942125-90-7 (Jan. 31, 2022)

"What is Messiah?" This book carries an important message of love and guidance to people living now from the Modern-Day Messiah or the Modern-Day Savior. It also reveals the secret of Shambhala, the spiritual center of Earth, as well as the truth that this spiritual center is currently in danger of perishing and what we can do to protect this sacred place. Discover the true love of God and the ideal practice of faith, here, in this book.

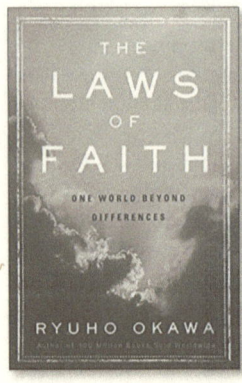

The Laws of Faith

One World Beyond Differences

Paperback • 208 pages • $15.95
ISBN: 978-1-942125-34-1 (Mar. 31, 2018)

In this book, Ryuho Okawa preaches the core teachings of the world religion and the faith in the God of Earth. By integrating logical and spiritual viewpoints, Okawa gives answers to modern-day problems that traditional religions cannot solve. Through this book, you will learn to go beyond different values, harmonize with each other and between nations, and create a world filled with peace and prosperity.

Other Books

An Unshakable Mind

How to Overcome Life's Difficulties

Paperback • 180 pages • $17.95
ISBN:978-1-942125-91-4 (Nov. 30, 2023)

This book will guide you to build the genuine self-confidence necessary to shape a resilient character and withstand life's turbulence. Ryuho Okawa breaks down the cause of life's difficulties and provides solutions to overcome them from the spiritual viewpoint of life based on the laws of the mind.

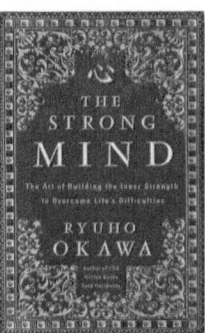

The Strong Mind

The Art of Building the Inner Strength to Overcome Life's Difficulties

Paperback • 192 pages • $15.95
ISBN: 978-1-942125-36-5 (May 25, 2018)

The Strong Mind is what we need to rise time and again and to move forward no matter what difficulties we face in life. This book will inspire and empower you to take courage, cultivate yourself, and achieve resilience and hardiness so that you can break through your limits and keep winning in the battle of your life.

The Essence of Buddha

The Path to Enlightenment

Paperback • 208 pages • $14.95
ISBN: 978-1-942125-06-8 (Oct. 1, 2016)

The essence of Shakyamuni Buddha's original teachings of the mind are explained in simple language: how to attain inner happiness, the wisdom to conquer ego, and the path to enlightenment for people in the contemporary era. It is a way of life that anyone can practice to achieve lifelong self-growth.

The Truth about Spiritual Phenomena
Life's Q&A with El Cantare

Paperback • 232 pages • $17.95
ISBN: 978-1-958655-0-92 (Oct. 27, 2023)

These are the records of Ryuho Okawa's answers to 26 questions related to spiritual phenomena and mental health, which were conducted live during his early public lectures with the audience. With his great spiritual ability, he revealed the unknown spiritual Truth behind the spiritual phenomena.

What Is Happy Science?
Best Selection of Ryuho Okawa's Early Lectures (Volume 1)

Paperback • 256 pages • $17.95
ISBN: 978-1-942125-99-0 (Aug. 25, 2023)

The Best Selection series is a collection of Ryuho Okawa's passionate lectures from the ages of 32 to 33 that reveal the mission and goal of Happy Science. This book contains the eternal Truth, including the meaning of life, the secret of the mind, the true meaning of love, the mystery of the universe, and how to end hatred and world conflicts.

The Road to Cultivate Yourself
Follow Your Silent Voice Within to Gain True Wisdom

Paperback • 200 pages • $17.95
ISBN: 978-1-958655-05-4 (Jun. 22, 2023)

In the age of uncertainty, how should we live our lives?

This book offers unchanging Truth in the ever-changing world, such as the secrets to becoming more aware of the spiritual self and how to increase intellectual productivity amidst the rapid changes of the modern age. It is packed with Ryuho Okawa's crystallized wisdom of life.

The True Eightfold Path

Guideposts for Self-Innovation

Paperback • 256 pages • $16.95
ISBN: 978-1-942125-80-8 (Mar. 30, 2021)

This book explains how we can apply the Eightfold Path, one of the main pillars of Shakyamuni Buddha's teachings, as everyday guideposts in the modern age to achieve self-innovation to live better and make positive changes in these uncertain times.

The Rebirth of Buddha

My Eternal Disciples, Hear My Words

Paperback • 280 pages • $17.95
ISBN: 978-1-942125-95-2 (Jul. 15, 2022)

These are the messages of Buddha who has returned to this modern age as promised to his eternal beloved disciples. They are in simple words and poetic style, yet contain profound messages. Once you start reading these passages, you will remember why you chose to be born in the same era as Buddha. Listen to the voices of your Eternal Master and awaken to your calling.

The Challenge of Enlightenment

Now, Here, the New Dharma Wheel Turns

Paperback • 380 pages • $17.95
ISBN: 978-1-942125-92-1 (Dec. 20, 2022)

Buddha's teachings, a reflection of his eternal wisdom, are like a bamboo pole used to change the course of your boat in the rapid stream of the great river called life. By reading this book, your mind becomes clearer, learns to savor inner peace, and it will empower you to make profound life improvements.

Words of Wisdom Series

Words for Life

Paperback • 136 pages • $15.95
ISBN: 979-8-88737-089-7 (Mar. 16, 2023)

Ryuho Okawa has written over 3,150 books on various topics. To help readers find the teachings that are beneficial for them out of the extensive teachings, the author has written 100 phrases and put them together. Inside you will find words of wisdom that will help you improve your mindset and lead you to live a meaningful and happy life.

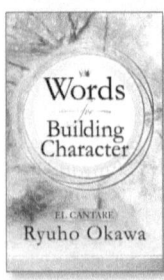

Words for Building Character

Paperback • 140 pages • $15.95
ISBN: 979-8-88737-091-0 (Jun. 21, 2023)

When your life comes to an end, what you can bring with you to the other world is your enlightenment, in other words, the character that you build in this lifetime. If you can read, relish, and truly understand the meaning of these religious phrases, you will be able to attain happiness that transcends this world and the next.

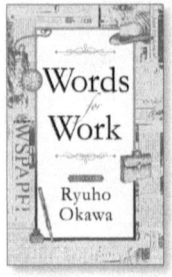

Words for Work

Paperback • 140 pages • $15.95
ISBN: 979-8-88737-090-3 (Jul. 20, 2023)

Through his personal experiences at work, Ryuho Okawa has created these phrases regarding philosophies and practical wisdom about work. This book will be of great use to you throughout your career. Every day you can contemplate and gain tips on how to better your work as well as deepen your insight into company management.

Words to Read in Times of Illness

Hardcover • 136 pages • $17.95
ISBN: 978-1-958655-07-8 (Sep. 15, 2023)

Ryuho Okawa has written 100 Healing Messages to comfort the souls of those going through any illness. When we are ill, it is an ideal time for us to contemplate recent and past events, as well as our relationship with the people around us. It is a chance for us to take inventory of our emotions and thoughts.

El Cantare Ryuho Okawa Original Songs

A song celebrating Lord God / With Savior

Words & Music by Ryuho Okawa

1. A song celebrating Lord God—Renewal ver.
2. With Savior —Renewal ver.
3. A song celebrating Lord God— Renewal ver. (Instrumental)
4. With Savior —Renewal ver. (Instrumental)
5. With Savior —Renewal ver. (Instrumental with chorus)

HAPPY SCIENCE'S ENGLISH SUTRA

"The True Words Spoken By Buddha"

"The True Words Spoken By Buddha" is an English sutra given directly from the spirit of Shakyamuni Buddha, who is a part of Master Ryuho Okawa's subconscious. The words in this sutra are not of a mere human being but are the words of God or Buddha sent directly from the ninth dimension, which is the highest realm of the Earth's Spirit World.

"The True Words Spoken By Buddha" is an essential sutra for us to connect and live with God or Buddha's Will as our own.

MEMBERSHIPS

MEMBERSHIP

If you would like to know more about Happy Science, please consider becoming a member. Those who pledge to believe in Lord El Cantare and wish to learn more can join us.

When you become a member, you will receive the following sutras: "The True Words Spoken By Buddha," "Prayer to the Lord" and "Prayer to Guardian and Guiding Spirits."

DEVOTEE MEMBER

If you would like to learn the teachings of Happy Science and walk the path of faith, become a Devotee member who pledges devotion to the Three Treasures, which are Buddha, Dharma, and Sangha. Buddha refers to Lord El Cantare, Master Ryuho Okawa. Dharma refers to Master Ryuho Okawa's teachings. Sangha refers to Happy Science. Devoting to the Three Treasures will let your Buddha nature shine, and you will enter the path to attain true freedom of the mind.

Becoming a devotee means you become Buddha's disciple. You will discipline your mind and act to bring happiness to society.

✉ **EMAIL** OR☎ **PHONE CALL**

Please turn to the contact information page.

🖥 **ONLINE** [member.happy-science.org/signup/ ⊚]

CONTACT INFORMATION

Happy Science is a worldwide organization with branches and temples around the globe. For a comprehensive list, visit the worldwide directory at happy-science.org. The following are some of our main Happy Science locations:

UNITED STATES AND CANADA

New York
79 Franklin St., New York, NY 10013, USA
Phone: 1-212-343-7972
Fax: 1-212-343-7973
Email: ny@happy-science.org
Website: happyscience-usa.org

New Jersey
66 Hudson St., #2R, Hoboken, NJ 07030, USA
Phone: 1-201-313-0127
Email: nj@happy-science.org
Website: happyscience-usa.org

Chicago
2300 Barrington Rd., Suite #400,
Hoffman Estates, IL 60169, USA
Phone: 1-630-937-3077
Email: chicago@happy-science.org
Website: happyscience-usa.org

Florida
5208 8th St., Zephyrhills, FL 33542, USA
Phone: 1-813-715-0000
Fax: 1-813-715-0010
Email: florida@happy-science.org
Website: happyscience-usa.org

Atlanta
1874 Piedmont Ave., NE Suite 360-C
Atlanta, GA 30324, USA
Phone: 1-404-892-7770
Email: atlanta@happy-science.org
Website: happyscience-usa.org

San Francisco
525 Clinton St.
Redwood City, CA 94062, USA
Phone & Fax: 1-650-363-2777
Email: sf@happy-science.org
Website: happyscience-usa.org

Los Angeles
1590 E. Del Mar Blvd., Pasadena,
CA 91106, USA
Phone: 1-626-395-7775
Fax: 1-626-395-7776
Email: la@happy-science.org
Website: happyscience-usa.org

Orange County
16541 Gothard St. Suite 104
Huntington Beach, CA 92647
Phone: 1-714-659-1501
Email: oc@happy-science.org
Website: happyscience-usa.org

San Diego
7841 Balboa Ave. Suite #202
San Diego, CA 92111, USA
Phone: 1-626-395-7775
Fax: 1-626-395-7776
E-mail: sandiego@happy-science.org
Website: happyscience-usa.org

Hawaii
Phone: 1-808-591-9772
Fax: 1-808-591-9776
Email: hi@happy-science.org
Website: happyscience-usa.org

Kauai
3343 Kanakolu Street, Suite 5
Lihue, HI 96766, USA
Phone: 1-808-822-7007
Fax: 1-808-822-6007
Email: kauai-hi@happy-science.org
Website: happyscience-usa.org

Toronto

845 The Queensway
Etobicoke, ON M8Z 1N6, Canada
Phone: 1-416-901-3747
Email: toronto@happy-science.org
Website: happy-science.ca

Vancouver

#201-2607 East 49th Avenue,
Vancouver, BC, V5S 1J9, Canada
Phone: 1-604-437-7735
Fax: 1-604-437-7764
Email: vancouver@happy-science.org
Website: happy-science.ca

INTERNATIONAL

Tokyo

1-6-7 Togoshi, Shinagawa,
Tokyo, 142-0041, Japan
Phone: 81-3-6384-5770
Fax: 81-3-6384-5776
Email: tokyo@happy-science.org
Website: happy-science.org

London

3 Margaret St.
London, W1W 8RE United Kingdom
Phone: 44-20-7323-9255
Fax: 44-20-7323-9344
Email: eu@happy-science.org
Website: www.happyscience-uk.org

Sydney

516 Pacific Highway, Lane Cove North,
2066 NSW, Australia
Phone: 61-2-9411-2877
Fax: 61-2-9411-2822
Email: sydney@happy-science.org

Sao Paulo

Rua. Domingos de Morais 1154,
Vila Mariana, Sao Paulo SP
CEP 04010-100, Brazil
Phone: 55-11-5088-3800
Email: sp@happy-science.org
Website: happyscience.com.br

Jundiai

Rua Congo, 447, Jd. Bonfiglioli
Jundiai-CEP, 13207-340, Brazil
Phone: 55-11-4587-5952
Email: jundiai@happy-science.org

Seoul

74, Sadang-ro 27-gil,
Dongjak-gu, Seoul, Korea
Phone: 82-2-3478-8777
Fax: 82-2-3478-9777
Email: korea@happy-science.org

Taipei

No. 89, Lane 155, Dunhua N. Road,
Songshan District, Taipei City 105, Taiwan
Phone: 886-2-2719-9377
Fax: 886-2-2719-5570
Email: taiwan@happy-science.org

Taichung

No. 146, Minzu Rd., Central Dist.,
Taichung City 400001, Taiwan
Phone: 886-4-22233777
Email: taichung@happy-science.org

Kuala Lumpur

No 22A, Block 2, Jalil Link Jalan Jalil Jaya
2, Bukit Jalil 57000,
Kuala Lumpur, Malaysia
Phone: 60-3-8998-7877
Fax: 60-3-8998-7977
Email: malaysia@happy-science.org
Website: happyscience.org.my

Kathmandu

Kathmandu Metropolitan City,
Ward No. 15, Ring Road, Kimdol,
Sitapaila Kathmandu, Nepal
Phone: 977-1-537-2931
Email: nepal@happy-science.org

Kampala

Plot 877 Rubaga Road, Kampala
P.O. Box 34130 Kampala, UGANDA
Email: uganda@happy-science.org

ABOUT HS PRESS

HS Press is an imprint of IRH Press Co., Ltd. IRH Press Co., Ltd., based in Tokyo, was founded in 1987 as a publishing division of Happy Science. IRH Press publishes religious and spiritual books, journals, and magazines and also operates broadcast and film production enterprises. For more information, visit *okawabooks.com*.

Follow us on:

f Facebook: Okawa Books   Instagram: OkawaBooks
▶ Youtube: Okawa Books   🐦 Twitter: Okawa Books
𝓟 Pinterest: Okawa Books   g Goodreads: Ryuho Okawa

——— **NEWSLETTER** ———

To receive book-related news, promotions and events, please subscribe to our newsletter below.

🔗 irhpress.com/pages/subscribe

——— **AUDIO / VISUAL MEDIA** ———

YOUTUBE

PODCAST

Introduction of Ryuho Okawa's titles; topics ranging from self-help, current affairs, spirituality, religion, and the universe.